The Little Book of Fishing

An Anthology

The Little Book of Fishing

INTRODUCTION BY NICK LYONS

EDITED BY WILL BALLIETT

A Balliett & Fitzgerald Book

ATLANTIC MONTHLY PRESS
NEW YORK

From Krissy and Dan - 6/5/02 Harding

Published simultaneously in Canada
Printed in the United States of America

Library of Congress Cataloging-in-Publication Data

The little book of fishing: an anthology / introduction by Nick Lyons;
edited by Will Balliett.
"A Balliett & Fitzgerald Book."
ISBN 0-87113-568-X
1. Fishing.   I. Balliett, Will.
SH441.L57   1994   799. 1—dc20   93-46760

DESIGN BY MICHAEL HARVEY

The Atlantic Monthly Press
841 Broadway
New York, NY 10003

FIRST PRINTING

Contents

Introduction

In my teens, in Brooklyn, my world was circumscribed by cement. The closest fishing was at Sheepshead Bay, near Coney Island, and mostly I fished through memory and through what I read in the five or six sporting magazines I bought each month. My narrow world of fishing included a bait-casting reel with a propensity for colossal backlashes, a cheap white glass rod, coarse line, three boxes of hooks, and a dozen lead sinkers, one to three ounces each. We used spearing or cut mackerel for bait when we fished fifty feet above the water on Steeplechase Pier, and night crawlers (which we'd plucked from local lawns) for trout, when we began to head north. To borrow Jean Shepherd's phrase, we were mostly "great vicarious anglers." We talked about fishing constantly; we went to sportsmen's shows and tackle shops; we ordered every free catalog remotely connected to fishing or camping that we found advertised. And we read.

Fishing was a thing I just did, which I'd always done, from before memory—something I'd always do. When I was four or five, fishing a little sump called Ice Pond (Revolutionary soldiers had taken ice from it) had saved me from the gray loneliness of a boarding school, the isolation, and had added adventure and suspense and a strong connection to the world beyond me, the natural world, when I was beginning to turn inward, ingrown, like a smashed toenail.

So I have always been grateful to fishing, happy with it as a part of my life, unable to explain its allure and unwilling, ever, to justify or apologize for it. And I have learned from it and have grown, both as a human being and as a fisherman, as I practiced more and more disciplined and exacting versions of the sport—bait-fishing, then spinning, and for years now mostly fly fishing—first near home, then far. I began to write about fishing quite late—in my mid-thirties, after a false start as a poet and too much academic writing. Writing about fishing gave me a new voice—earthy, humorous, with far more energy and animation than I'd been able to use in any of the thirty-odd critical essays I'd written for the little literary magazines, or my scholarly book. So I'm grateful to it for that, too.

I know I read Hemingway's "Big Two-Hearted River" in my early twenties, though not as a "fishing" story, but when I first began to read literature widely and intensely. Most of the other work I read on the sport came from magazines; what I read in Brooklyn let me fish from Argentina to New Zealand with men like Lee Wulff, Joe Brooks, A. J. McClane, and a host of others, and I learned certain practical skills and techniques from writers like "Tap" Tapply. But only when I became a book editor did I begin to look at the vast expanse of writing that had been done on fishing. At first I looked for practical books that I thought should be back in print. *Art Flick's Streamside Guide* was first, and it led me to Preston Jennings, Ernest Schwiebert, Alfred Ronalds, Vincent Marinaro, and a raft of others, several of whom I was able to republish. A fellow editor gave me Edward R. Hewitt's wonderful memoir *A Trout and Salmon Fisherman for Seventy-five Years*—the first of its kind I'd ever read. I found McGuane's early novels, with their superb fishing scenes. I read the stories and essays written about the sport in much the same way as I'd done for my scholarship and college teaching: all of an author I'd "discovered" and could find, all at once. Then, in the late 1960s I wrote my first fishing narrative, showed the printed version to doormen and maiden aunts and colleagues, then promptly wrote another, and then edited a large fishing anthology that drew me even deeper into the heart of the matter.

My old friend Sparse Grey Hackle—whose *Fishless Days, Angling Nights* I was preparing for publication—told me something one day that he'd written elsewhere: The finest fishing often takes place not on water but in print.

And so it does, as this brief and balanced little book will show you. Its selections are wonderfully varied, with fourteen distinctly different voices and visions, well-chosen by editor Will Balliett and photography editor f-stop Fitzgerald; I'm honored to have my old story "Mecca" included in such company. The pieces are narrative, reflective, wise, humorous, tense, philosophical, or some combination of the above. They tell what happened to the author (more or less—because fishermen, as Ed Zern once said, are born honest but they get over it) and they tell what it all means, at least to them. They create memorable scenes that will engage non-fishermen along with the initiate, and they explore—often with pungent wit—the absurdities that sometimes gather around any sport with passionate participants. Among the men and women in this fine company of anglers, you'll find a poet, some novelists, a variety of essayists, several theorists, an editorial-page editor, and a major sportswriter. The fishing is pretty good, too—from big largemouth bass in a southern swamp to Chilean trout that remind Red Smith of Two-ton Tony Galento and Jane Russell. And the book is chock-full of surprises.

As you fish through the selections, you'll see a number of themes emerge—chiefly initiation and connection. Fishing of all stripes—though perhaps most often fly fishing—begins with sudden, often dramatic, revelations of what it's all about, and it continues with an incrementing passion. It draws lives together, helps to build new friendships, creates closer relationships within a family; and it draws us, always, closer to a connection with the natural world, especially the part embodied in or near water. And its meaning, if it indeed has one (or two or three), eludes us and goads us at the very moments when it cries out most for definition.

John Cole discovers fishing and sex on the same day; Le Anne Schreiber develops an abiding link with her father, to the sport he loves most, fly fishing, and to the places where it is practiced; Jean Shepherd, through a crazy night of fishing on a northern Indiana lake, passes through the portal to adulthood; Thomas McGuane shows us the relationship between father and daughter revealed and enhanced by a day astream together. People discover stuff about themselves that they didn't know; they learn about others in a new way; and they discover where human beings stand in relation to rivers and lakes, and their denizens. Some of the authors speculate mightily on what animates this passion, long after people have had to fish for food—why they like it and in what ways.

This is a happy, sprightly collection—full of wonder, discovery, fun, wit, philosophy, memoir, and much of the best that can be called "piscatorial prose." You cannot come away from *The Little Book of Fishing* without feeling grateful for the glimpses into a panoply of other lives, for the revelations and the laughter.

This is probably not the last book you will want to read about fishing, but it's certainly a fine initiation to a world that is diverse and full, that gives its own brand of pleasure: the fishing in print.

NICK LYONS

East Hampton, August 28, 1939

John N. Cole

*First loves—romantic or piscatorial—take many forms, some odd, some full of
revelation, most full of passion. In the tangled skein of firsts in this
hilarious and memorable chapter from* Fishing Came First, *John Cole
makes discoveries that change his life, both on
and off the water. Keep your eyes on the sand eels and blowfish.*
—NL

I am the Blanche DuBois of fishermen. I have always depended on the kindness of strangers.

Wyman Aldrich is not a total stranger, but he is in his early sixties and I am sixteen. The two age groups are seldom paired, unless the older is an uncle, grandfather, or guardian; in either case the adolescent involved is likely to be cynical about the chances of finding true happiness with any adult male.

But fishing can change everything, life included.

There is a confluence of elements here on Long Island's East End in late August and early September that creates crystal air. As summer glides toward the autumnal equinox and high pressure builds in the heavens, certain mornings become complete units of hours suspended, as if nature has succeeded in generating a timeless moment, a shimmering souvenir of a passing season, saved and pinned in the book of elements, motionless, perfect, intoxicating, and touched with the tragedy of its own fragility.

This is such a morning. Its glories drape me like Joseph's coat as I stand at the very edge of the East Hampton Town Dock peering down at schools of silversides, gathered in trembling, emerald circles, throbbing with the panic of their knowledge that they are being watched by this year's crop of adolescent bluefish, the half-pound snappers, already perfect replicas of their savage parents. And, just as those parents slash hapless schools of menhaden to a water-borne melange of blood, guts, and scales, so do these miniatures emulate more massacres. Only the scale differs: instead of dicing one-pound menhaden as their parents do, snappers granulate silversides about as long as my index finger.

As I watch, a silverside school of at least three hundred fish congeals to a sphere as compact as a cannonball. Each individual struggles to find the center of the mass and to stay there, hoping that when a snapper strikes, the outer minnows will be the first to go. The tighter the sphere, the closer their doom. The one I watch is so congealed, I expect it to sink.

From the depths of the Three Mile Harbor channel that flows dark past the dock, a small shape accelerates, aquamarine and silver in the clear waters of this crystal day. Hurtling directly at the silverside sphere, the snapper produces what for him must be a gratifying panic.

The cannonball explodes, becomes an underwater pyrotechnic display as elaborate as any Fourth of July extravaganza. Tiny shooting stars zoom in every direction, filling the underwater sky. Others surface. In concert, on this still morning, the sound of their surfacing is the hiss of a cotton sheet being ripped end to end. Remarkable.

I am fully fascinated. Totally absorbed. Watching fish is, for me, an infallible pastime, more delightful than masturbation, infinitely more enjoyable than tennis lessons, swimming, lunch at the beach, or sailing races at Devon: each the primary recreational activities our parents, as they continue to remind us, have worked so hard to make possible during our summer holidays on this graceful sand spit between the Sound and the sea 125 miles east of the city where I was born.

Somehow, Wyman Aldrich has recognized my proclivity. Perhaps he and my parents have discussed my odd recreational choice. (I can hear my mother wondering aloud why I'm not on the tennis courts with my friends, or the chosen teenagers she hopes will be my friends.) But although Wyman belongs to the same club, he is not a frequent attender. His wife and my grandmother sit and chat under the awning of Granny's cabana, but Wyman is most often absent.

He has, it turns out, gone fishing.

And somewhere in the course of his nonfishing hours, he has learned I am a fisherman too.

So, on this opalescent forenoon as he pilots his boat past Three Mile's frequent channel markers from her berth at the head of the harbor, he spots me on the Town Dock, fish-watching.

Turning the boat toward the dock, he waves. I return the greeting; I know who he is, but I do not feel that I know him and I wonder if it is I that he approaches. Perhaps, I think, he wants to pick up a lobster or two from Emerson Taber, whose boat and lobster pound occupy the southwest corner of the point of land I'm standing on.

"John," calls Wyman as he gets close enough to be heard over the pop-pop of the one-lung inboard chugging at the center of his sixteen-foot skiff, "come on along. I'm going out in the bay for a little fishing."

How glorious the moment of my acceptance. It is, beyond any doubt, the purest verification of my tenuous independence. The simple, trembling act of clambering down the pilings to set foot aboard Wyman's waiting boat is as overpowering for me as Mark Antony's first step aboard Cleopatra's barge must have been for him.

Wyman's boat is comfortable and complete, deceptively simple. From the Town Dock, she appeared to be a straight forward skiff: gray, wooden, the sort of open boat that frequents a thousand harbors. But as I step aboard I realize this boat is strip-built, and with great care. She is not a flat-bottomed sharpy banged together over a winter in some Bonnacker's garage; this boat's bow flares, her curves flow, and her prim V-bottom is finely fashioned to turn aside short seas instead of being slapped by them.

Mounted amidships, the one-lung Palmer engine is a museum piece. Its massive flywheel could anchor a ferry, and each of its brass petcocks, valves, and fittings are golden bright in the sun. From stem to stern, everything aboard this boat is cared for.

Like Wyman. His skin is as tanned and sea-cured as that of any commercial fisherman. A thin veil of age sifts the blueness of his eyes, and wrinkles wreathe his neck where it meets the collar of his open, faded shirt. But his face—that great, sagging, weatherbeaten, wonderful face—is alive with Wyman's bright and boyish spirit. I look into his eyes and there is all the mischief, the excitement, and the rebellion that I feel as I come aboard: free, gone for the day, escaped, without even asking or telling anyone where I am going or who I am with.

"Take a seat," Wyman says, "up forward." He sits in the stern, steering with a tiller mounted on the gunwale: push it forward and the boat heads to starboard; pull, and she turns to port.

Following the narrow channel, we pass the long breakwater of granite blocks, peopled now with fishermen, most of them with the bamboo poles favored here for snapper fishing. Just add fifteen or twenty feet of line, a snelled hook baited with a silverside, swing it into the tide and soon you can do battle with twelve ounces of scrappy snapper: the best of breakfasts, quickly browned in butter the next morning. Until this adventure, the breakwater has been my only boat. Today I wave to my fellow land-bound anglers as we pass; I am tolerant of the less fortunate.

Past the blinking light at the breakwater's end we turn east, following the shore along Hog Creek inlet, headed for the buoy at Lion's Head Rock where the land corners and falls away to the south, toward Napeague's low dunes, the slim finger of sand that separates the Atlantic from Gardiner's Bay. Where the dunes bend just east of Devon, the smokestacks of the fish-meal factory rise; the channel we follow is deep enough to accommodate the high-bowed, 140-foot bunker steamers that pursue the same menhaden as do the bluefish, net them by the thousands of tons, and steam, gunwales at the water line, to the factory to unload countless flattened fish from their oily holds on conveyors that carry the carcasses to stinking vats where the menhaden are pressed like over ripe, silver grapes and oil spills from them to be refined to a fine and delicate lubricant.

The squashed remains are loaded into great drying ovens and the flaky residue of bones and flesh ground into fish meal measured into one hundred-pound burlap bags carried, still hot, on the backs of black workers to waiting box cars.

Wyman and I are not thinking of fish as industrial raw material; for us, they are the pivot of our exhilarating freedom and we worship them.

We anchor a few hundred feet off the high, rust-colored cliffs of sand that rise from the shore to the Bell Estate, a place I have never set foot and knew little of until this view from the water. Now I can see the shingled mansion at the cliff's tops, the covered stairway with its electrically powered chair that rides a bannister so visitors to the pier below will not have to make the climb on foot. Mr. Bell, which is all I have ever heard him called, is rich. That much I know. But he has no fishing boat at his dock, and there are rumors that he keeps to himself in the house, tended by a nurse reported to be his mistress.

If I were rich, and lived here, I tell myself, I would fish every day.

Wyman opens several clams, letting juice drip over his fingers, separating the meat from the shells and dropping the flesh into a coffee can he has half-filled with bay water.

"Got these earlier this morning," he says, "near Sammi's Beach. Just waded in and dug them out with my feet. Ever do that, John?"

"No sir," I say, telling myself I'll be sure to try tomorrow.

"There. Now, pass me those two rods and we'll pay a call on Mr. Fish."

I hand Wyman the two stiff, rather stubby, black metal boat rods. Each is fitted with a Pflueger spool reel loaded with stout Cuttyhunk line ending in a stiff gut leader made fast to two hooks, one above the other, and a four-ounce, pyramid,

13

lead sinker.

Taking a slice of raw clam from the coffee can, Wyman threads it onto one of the hooks. "Put some of this foot meat on," he explains. "It's tough, hard to steal.

"Then, on the other, we'll give those fish plenty of gooslum. Take this juicy stuff here, this part that runs along the edge of the shell, and hook it through a couple of times at one end." His brown, blunt fingers caress a flimsy strand of clam that reminds me of what I find in my handkerchief after I sneeze.

"There," he says. "See how that gooslum hangs off the hook. In the water, that behaves like a worm wriggling. A worm, or maybe a sand eel. Fish just love it.

"Here." He hands me a rod with both hooks baited.

"Drop the line down until you feel the sinker hit bottom, then reel in just enough so the sinker bumps when you move your rod tip up and down."

Tentatively, eyeing Wyman as he works his rod, I release the reel's brake. The bottom seems a long, dark ways down as line slips through the guides. I try to imagine how the bait looks now that it has left the sunlight to swim in the invisible mystery so far beneath us.

Bump. I feel a soft thud along the rod as tension leaves the line. Wyman, who is watching, says, "That's bottom. Now reel in just a bit. Get the line tight.

"Ahh," he says after a minute or so, "there's Mr. Fish. A touch. I have a touch, and another." He laughs.

I think to myself, he must have dropped his line right on top of a fish.

But Wyman is not moving his hands. He sits there, intent, his eyes on the moving tip of his rod, bowing now, bending just a bit.

Wyman grunts as the tip bends sharply; then he rares back, lifting the rod much more vigorously than I expected.

"Well, hello there," he says. "Hello, hello, hello."

He is turning the crank handle on his reel, retrieving line slowly, steadily, enjoying every moment, laughing, savoring for surely the thousandth time this summer, this first meeting of the day with his friend, the fish, a friend he talks to throughout their acquaintance.

"Come on, now, don't leave me now, not without a look. I know you're not too big, but you could make a nice meal. And I want John to see you. You don't feel like a flounder, not like a weakfish. I think I know what you are. Yes, I do. I think I know you, Mr. Fish.

"Well bless my soul," says Wyman, as he lifts up his rod and swings a small, brown-and-white grotesque dumpling of a fish into the boat. "You're a blow-fish. A blowfish.

"Ever meet Mr. Blowfish, John?"

I shake my head, staring at the creature.

Picking it up, holding it in his hand like a potato, Wyman wiggles the hook free, carefully. He pushes the fish toward me. "Here, look here," he says, point-ing at the strange, small face peering from the circle of Wyman's fingers and thumb.

"Pay attention to these teeth, John. These are teeth that bite, and they are strong enough to do damage." I see four teeth, two up, two down. They look like the teeth cartoonists put in chipmunks' mouths: flat, wide, curved just a bit. Teeth for a rodent, not a fish.

"And look at these eyes. A blowfish has green eyes. Can you believe it."

The eyes I see are almond-shaped, almost oblong, set close above what ought to be a blowfish nose, even though I know fish don't have noses. But this one has no gills, not that I can see. This fish appears to be all head, with a shape like a foreshortened, mottled, brown eggplant, with four teeth and two green eyes at the fat end, and a tapering, short body that ends in a flimsy tail flapping aimlessly against Wyman's wrist.

"Watch this, John."

Turning the blowfish over, Wyman reveals its white belly, a white so pale it is luminous. With his index finger, he scratches the belly, gently, almost a tickle. Making sounds I never anticipated, short grunts and grinding of those teeth, the blowfish begins to swell. First, its belly, like a large blister, then the entire body inflates, taut, rigid, under internal pressures that startle me. The skin that seemed almost slimy when the blowfish came from the water has been transformed; now it is rough, bristling with a thousand tiny spines that are coarse sandpaper on my fingertips as I rub the pale belly.

What Wyman holds is no longer a fish, but a near-perfect sphere, a large grapefruit with a tummy taut enough to drum. Heaving the softball into the air,

15

Wyman laughs as the creature arcs against our perfect autumnal sky.

When it hits the water, the blowfish floats for a split second, a small buoy in the channel. Then, with a quick burble, it deflates and is gone.

"Too small to keep," Wyman says. "But his big brothers and sisters are still down there. You better check your line, John. You haven't been paying attention to your fishing."

He's right. When I reel in, both my hooks are bare.

We catch six keepers in the next half-hour, throw back as many small ones. It's all blowfish today; no weakfish, no fluke, not even a skate.

Wyman asks, "Want some lunch?" I say yes and wait for him to reach into one of his knapsacks for a sandwich or crackers, but he asks me to haul in the anchor and when I do he starts the Palmer and heads for Cartwright Shoal.

About a mile to the east of our fishing spot, Cartwright is little more than a large sand bar just high enough above water to allow beach grass to get a grip. Separated from Gardiner's Island by a shoal and turbulent channel not more than a half-mile wide, Cartwright was probably part of the island a thousand years ago. Some treasure hunters are certain it was; they claim Captain Kidd buried a good part of his loot somewhere on Gardiner's, and they say Cartwright is one of the most likely spots. No treasure has ever been found, but over at the fish factory store where oil coats, hooks, tarred line, and boots are sold to commercial fishermen, there is plenty of talk about gill netters and trap fishermen who have found gold coins in the Cartwright sand.

To my knowledge, no one has ever seen an actual coin on display, however.

Like two pirates, Wyman and I wade ashore after he nudges the bow of his skiff into soft sand on Cartwright's south shore. We carry equipment and supplies Wyman pulled from the cuddy as we neared the island: a wire grill, knife, bread board, skillet, two bottles of ginger ale, and a small slab of salt pork wrapped in waxed paper. I decide there's no guessing how much stuff Wyman has packed into that small space under the forward deck.

After we get organized, I go back to the skiff for the bucket that holds the blowfish. Wyman has already started a small fire built from the driftwood that litters much of Cartwright.

Taking one blowfish at a time from the bucket, he holds it belly down on the bread board and makes a deep cut behind its head. Then he works his thumb under the skin of the back half, holds tight to the head, and yanks the skin from the whole rear part of the fish. A tapering, pearly chunk of meat emerges, as innocent as a newborn. It's about four inches long and I would never have guessed such an odd-looking fish could give birth to such a morsel.

Wyman puts the six pearls into the hot skillet, already popping with a couple of chunks of salt pork, tosses some pepper, and keeps the morsels moving with his knife blade. Meanwhile, herring gulls are having a screaming time of it with the blowfish guts and heads we left for them at the water's edge.

Every moment of this pageant of preparation is new to me. Never before have I seen fish caught, cleaned, and cooked within an hour. Never before have I smelled the magic of salt pork in a frying pan over an open fire flickering on a pirate island where we are the only two humans for miles. Wyman Aldrich has made this possible. He is supposed to be having lunch by the club pool with his wife and my grandmother; they are there at this moment, shaking their heads at the old man's ornery independence. I decide then and there that Wyman Aldrich is my hero, the person I want to become. For this day he has raised the curtain on a watery stage set with wonders, wonders that wait for me.

Sitting here on an ancient ship's timber too heavy for anything but a hurricane to have brought to Cartwright, pushing hot flakes of sweet and fragrant white, fresh fish into my mouth, tasting the salt pork's tang and relishing the woodsmoke on the enchanted equinoctial air, I know with infinite certainty that I have found the fulcrum of my future. A boat, a fishing rod and reel, and the knowledge to guide me to the fullest realization of their potential for adventure —this is what life holds for me, out there in the coming of age that I have, until this day, viewed with such skeptical anxiety.

Sweeping from horizon to horizon is the setting of my years, caught here in the piercing clarity of this instant: Montauk Point off to the northeast, Hither Hills rising dark to the east, Napeague's slim fingers of sand, the pushing stacks of the fish factory, the white pickets of the yacht club dock, Bell's mansion on the rusty cliffs, Lion's Head Rock, and off to the northwest, the smudge of Connecticut across the Sound, blending with Fisher's Island and pulling in to the green woods of Gardiner's Island just over my shoulder. I am surrounded by the salt sea and the land that frames it in this magnificent meeting of the two. Today, the world spins about me waiting to take me aboard.

When Wyman unloads me back at the Town Dock in the weighty silence of a still midafternoon, I have no words of proper gratitude. What can I tell him? I can barely cope with the massive import of the day's unfolding. There are such moments: even in the midst of my clumsy, fumbling, pubescent years I perceive the worth of this August episode. I know, I truly do know as I wave to Wyman, standing, steering up the channel in the stern of his skiff with the sun over his shoulder, that he has, this day, given me a gift whose dimensions will take a life-time to decipher.

And, incredibly, my day is not over.

In the evening the older sister of a summer neighbor down the road tele-phones. She may be, for all I know, eighteen or even more. She has her own car, but we have scarcely spoken through the summer; she was there, that's all, when my brother Chick and I went to visit her younger brother, for touch foot-ball, or a bike ride to the village where we would sit at the White's Drug Store soda fountain assuaging our adolescence with sundaes swathed in chocolate and topped with powdered malted milk. "Dustys," we called them.

"Come on over," she says. "I'm all alone. Ned is off to school and my parents are in town."

It is dusk as I ride my bike the quarter-mile along Apaquogue Road to the place her parents rent for the summer. My heart is a pheasant beating short wings against my chest; my mouth is dry as powdered malted milk. What does she want? What is expected of me? What is not expected of me?

She, on the other hand, is absolutely in control. There is a smile in her eyes, a perfect equanimity in every comment. Jesus, she is old. Tall, in a white, pleated linen skirt with a cashmere sweater across her shoulders, her dark hair and blue eyes swimming over crimsoned lips against her summer-tanned cheeks, she says, "Let's go for a ride."

It is her own car, a maroon Ford coupe. She is the only girl I know with her own car, and I don't suppose I really know her.

She drives east, through the village, past Amagansett, on to the Montauk Highway as the night spins by us under cold stars hung from a moonless sky.

From the highest of the Hither Hills I can look northwest and see the pale sheet of Gardiner's Bay unfolding toward Connecticut; I am looking at the very seascape of the day's discoveries. It is this air, I tell myself, this electric equinoctial air. I am under a spell, lifted into the pages of a book more compelling than any I have ever read.

When we reach the Montauk Light, she prowls the parking lots until we find a place that overlooks the Atlantic and the Sound, that turbulent meeting place of perpetual tides.

But no more turbulent than our encounter. Enfolding me against her cashmere, she presses her lips to mine. Her tongue is a hot, darting sand eel, exploring every cavern of my esophagus, wriggling, alive inside me.

This is a first. I am electrified, jolted, slammed without pity into an encounter with passion. Stunned, totally stunned, motionless, I cannot respond, not for a while.

Then, as the blowfish in my corduroys swells to the rigidity of structural steel, I ask my own cruller of a tongue to try to catch up with the sand eel swimming in my mouth. My hands fumble aimlessly at cashmere.

Perhaps it is twenty minutes, even half an hour, before she ends the exercise. For me, it is an eternity. But she pulls back, as coolly as if she were changing courts in a tennis match, turns the ignition key, steps on the starter, and off we roll toward home.

No matter how I fashion my halting words, I cannot find the formula that will extend the evening. "Good night, Johnny," she says as we stand at her door. "I've got to get some sleep. Tomorrow morning I leave for the city."

I ease aching loins aboard my bike and pedal home, pondering the miracles this day has wrought.

No girl ever called me "Johnny" before.

But I go to sleep remembering Wyman.

Mecca

Nick Lyons

*"Mecca" was the second fishing narrative I wrote. This story came in response
to a trip I made from Woodstock to Roscoe with Frank Mele
and Jim Mulligan. Frank, today at eighty, still is the kind of rare fly-fishing
guru each of us needs. The trip took place twenty-five years ago and I
can see that it registers how I lost my heart to fly fishing forever.*
—NL

*Mecca (mĕk´á), n. 1. a holy city; hence, any place sought, especially
by great numbers of persons, as a supremely desirable goal.*

One spring there was no spring. March lingered into mid-April; late April was a wintry February; and by the end of May you might have been convinced that, since not even the Quill Gordon had arrived, God was taking a special vengeance on fly fishers. On all except me.

Emergence dates would be postponed; few trout would be taken in the fly-only stretches I had begun to haunt; June (unless God became ungodly vengeful toward fly-fishers) would be perfect. While small clusters of distressed anglers grumbled in the tackle shops, I gloated. June was the only time I would be free, and June would be ideal. Even Brannigan was morose. I was serenely gleeful.

All winter I had corresponded from the city with Mike, a fanatic like myself but one who had taken the plunge and now lived chiefly—and blissfully—for fishing. What other way is there? Brannigan constantly wrote me of his friend Hawkes, a knowledgeable old Catskill trouting genius whom I had never met. But Hawkes was more than knowledgeable, more than a rumor: he was a myth. In an increasing number of understated and sometimes unconscious ways, the old trout fisher—in off-seasons, a cellist—began to emerge from Mike's letters as a figure of outrageous proportions. He had, so far as I could tell, a special formula for dyeing leaders to within a chromophore of the color of eight different streams at a dozen different times of the year. He no longer kept emergence tables, but could tell (by extrasensory perception?) not only which fly would be hatching on a particular day, but at what time of the day, even to the hour, the fly would emerge. And in what numbers! Of course I believed none of it. Who would? It was all the fiction of that wild Irishman. Brannigan was obviously a madman, more afflicted even than I, who had lost two jobs because of his trout neurosis, and almost a wife: he was given to exaggeration, fantasy, mirage, and fly-tying. I had only almost lost my wife.

But I was curious. Who wouldn't be? And I had asked four or five times, covertly, whether or not Hawkes would fish with us when I got away for a week in June.

"Rarely fishes any more," wrote Brannigan. "Most streams have become rather easy for him; most hatches too pedestrian. Says he only fishes the Green Drake hatches—says there's still something to be learned there."

The Green Drake, yes—the most exciting and mysterious of them all. *Ephemera guttulata Pictet*, yes, which brought the junkers, the old soaks, out of the deep pools, which emerged in massive and manic hatches, sometimes for only a few days, perhaps a week. Sometimes the circus occurred on the Beaverkill as early as the first week in June, but sometimes, according to water temperatures no doubt, it was delayed for several weeks. Yes, to fish the Green Drake hatch on the Beaverkill this year with Hawkes, that was an ambition worth the four months of brooding and scheming. To return to the Beaverkill, which I had not fished in ten years, with the old myth himself, yes it would be Mecca, a vision to hold me throughout another long dry city winter.

But there was no adequate imitation of *Ephemera guttulata*—that was common knowledge. White Wulffs took a few fish; dyed light-green hackle flies took some; the attempts at exact imitation took very few; and, in the spinner stage, there was the adequate waxy-white and funereal Coffin Fly.

So I experimented that spring, to wile away the wait, and finally, in mid-May, accomplished what to my mind was a major innovation, a contribution to the angling fraternity of staggering proportions. I called it the Pigeon Drake, for the pigeon quill body I had used after a long quill had fluttered down to me, quite mystically, at the very moment I was thinking about this fly one dreary lunch hour. That quill was a portent, and I promptly sent my two older sons out to collect me several dozen in the park at a penny a quill. They brought in ninety-seven, but I used only thirty in my experiments and ultimately made only four or five usable flies.

The result is hard to describe. It was not a small fly, nor a particularly neat fly. The tip of the quill, through which I had inserted exactly three stems of stripped badger hackle for the tail had to be strapped firmly to the shank of the #12 hook. Peering up through specially purchased contact lenses from the bottom of a filled bathtub at numerous flies floating there (the door had to be locked to keep out my skeptical wife and distracting children), I observed that the white impala wings of the Wulff flies, sparsely tied, closely resembled the translucent wings of the Green Drake (and many other flies, which perhaps explains part of its extraordinary success). I dyed pure white hackle in green tea. The pigeon quill body, however, is what made the fly: it was natural, translucent, and would cock slightly upward if properly strapped to the shank. Frankly, it was the work of genius, and I could not wait to fish it with Mike and Hawkes on the Beaverkill—Mecca.

But it rained the first three days of my week's vacation, and all I could do was take Brannigan's abuse to the effect that a man who had not been out on the streams once by June ninth was a fallen man, fallen indeed, a man given over to mercantilism and paternalism and other such crimes and moral diseases as were destroying the world, or at least a noble sport. "These are dangerous years for you, Nick," he advised me. "Worse will lead to worse."

The fourth day was Brannigan's one day of work, his one day of homage to mercantilism and paternalism, and since Hawkes was not to be heard from (apparently he had disappeared), I went out glumly to a small mountain stream nearby and surprised myself by having a delightful day catching seven-and eight-inch brookies and browns on tiny #18 and #20 Cahills and Adamses, dry. It was fun watching the spirited streaks of trout shoot out of their cover and gulp the little flies; it was real sport handling them on 6X tippets. But it was not Mecca.

That night I could bear it no longer. Indirections lead to indirections, and I, a mercantilist, had no business being subtle. "Mike," I said, "it's the tenth of June. There have been no reports that the Green Drake hatch has started and it's due momentarily. Don't you have any idea where Hawkes is? Can't you simply hunt him up and ask him if he'll go to the Beaverkill with us tomorrow?"

Brannigan roared. "Sure. I know where Hawkes is. But you just don't ask him like that. It takes some engineering, and some luck. He's got to ask you."

"Dammit. What is he, Mike, a saint?"

Mike smiled and sipped at his fourth beer.

"Did you make the damn guy up?"

"All right. All right. I suppose I can find him. But I can't promise a thing."

Two days later, the night before I had to leave, after two days of mediocre fishing in the Esopus, Brannigan said simply, "Hawkes is going tomorrow; said we could come if we want to."

I tried to answer calmly. Though I still didn't believe a word about Hawkes, not a word of it, a myth is a myth, and it comes with ineluctable power, a power elusive and haunting.

The next morning at eight o'clock Brannigan was at his garage arranging his tackle, selecting from his six fly rods the best for the day.

"Hawkes thinks there might be a Green Drake hatch this evening," the bright white-haired Irishman said, "but that there might not."

Already a hedge; the tricks of the prophets, the ambiguities of the mediums. He didn't exist. Not the Hawkes I'd dreamed about.

Then, as I got out my gear and piled it beside Brannigan's, Hawkes arrived in his forty-six Dodge. His gaunt, lined face was that of a saint, or of a gunman. His eyes were deep set, limned with shadowy black globes; his fingers were long and thin and obviously arthritic. He walked stiffly toward us.

"Brannigan, old Branny, so this is our young friend," he said, extending his bony hand. "Has he made all the adequate preparations? If he is to be admitted into our little club, he must agree to will his ashes to us, that we may sprinkle them upon the waters of the Beaverkill."

Brannigan tried to suppress a smile. I tried, gently, to remove my hand from Hawkes' firm but friendly grasp.

"The Beaverkill," he continued, looking warmly at me, smiling, "home of Gordon and Darbee and Dette: Mecca. Tell me, Nick, do you face the Beaverkill every morning and every evening at sunset? Do you pray to the gods?"

"Of course he does, Hawkes," said Mike. "Now let's get started. This will be his only real day of trout fishing for the year."

"Very curious," said Hawkes, shaking his head. "One day of trout fishing. I'm sure our young friend has the burdens of the world upon him, then. Nevertheless, one day of real fishing can be enough. Especially at Mecca. It can be made to serve the whole of the year."

I smiled, an embarrassed, naive smile that spread and spread all day, until my cheeks hurt, on that long unforgettable drive to Mecca.

The drive to the Beaverkill should have taken no more than an hour. It was nine o'clock, and I had all hopes of catching the late-morning rise. But it took about an hour for us merely to pack Hawkes' old Dodge, an immaculate, impeccably ordered vehicle, with each object in its proper place: rods, waders, vest, extra fly boxes, net, and Jack Daniels whisky. There was a holder for his pipe above the dashboard, disposal bags, and four cans of beer neatly packed into the ample glove compartment. Hawkes placed each of our items of equipment carefully into the car, with such measured movements that he might have been giving them permanent homes. As he picked up each piece of tackle he would contemplate it for a moment and then comment on its appropriateness to the sport. "Branny, you know that felt is best for the Beaverkill—and yet you bring hobnails. Curious. Is there a special reason for that, Branny? Do you know something you're not telling? Have reports reached you of great mountains of silt and mud being washed into it? You surely would not be using them simply to impress the pedestrian likes of Nick and me, to taunt us with the fruit of some large sale of flies to a posh New York City tackle shop?"

And then, when the felt waders were brought out from Brannigan's garage, after another five minutes of slow, meticulous scrutiny, "I suppose you know that the glue you've used won't last the day. But the Irish are knowledgeable men, and if you've failed to use the preparation I gave you last winter, I'm sure you have your reasons."

At eleven we set out. Too late for the morning rise, but still early enough for a long day on the river. We wouldn't even have to stop for lunch, I thought, hopefully: pick up a sandwich or two for the vest, and hit the stream as soon as possible. I had a raging fever to be on the stream.

The old Dodge scrunched slowly out of Brannigan's pebbled driveway, made the semicircle onto the tarred road, and started, with incredible slowness, west— to Mecca.

Hawkes opened and closed his long arthritic fingers slowly around the wheel. "This is a day not to be rushed," he said. "It is going to be an experience, an event. It must be savored."

"Come off it, Hawkes," said Brannigan.

Hawkes stopped the car abruptly. Smack in the middle of the highway. Without taking his eyes away from the windshield in front of him, he said, with dead seriousness: "If this is to be a day of cynicism, of doubt, of feverish behavior by an unruly Irishman, I would be glad to turn around, return said Irishman to his own car, and make my peace elsewhere. I have my doubts that the Green Drakes will appear anyway; the temperature dropped to fifty-two degrees night before last—which, I take it, the less sensitive scholars of the streams *did not notice*—the barometer is failing, if slowly, and the moon was not to be seen last night. My fingers are tight, I have a telltale itch along my right thigh, and this *could* become a highly dubious proposition all the way around."

"Okay, okay, Hawkes. I apologize. Please—let's go."

"You're tense, man. Sink into the day. Don't force it. The electricity of such feverish thinking is transmuted imperceptibly but ineluctably to Mr. Brown Trout. The result you can well guess."

My smile spread, my cheeks ached. Three miles down the road Hawkes stopped at a gas station, got out, and asked the attendant about the composition of the gasoline. Hawkes got a drop on his fingers, smelled it, touched it gently to his lips, smiled, and wiped his fingers carefully on some paper toweling. "It is quite possible after all, gentlemen, that the Green Drake *will* make his appearance this afternoon. Very curious."

We started out again, and this time Hawkes was silent, thoughtful, meditative for five minutes. Several times he stopped the car at small mountain creeks, got out of the car, scrutinized the water, threw boysenberries into the eddies, and began to hum quietly. "Boys," he said, nodding, "it's really going to be a day. This is going to be an event."

Three more miles down the road, feeling immeasurably dry, he had to get a small bracer at a roadside tavern. We each ended having three tall beers apiece. Another mile, feeling too wet, he had to relieve himself, and did so in a conspicuously high arc. Half a mile farther and he stopped abruptly, whistled a long clear whistle, and watched a blonde farmgirl carrying a child walk slowly across a field of knee-high corn shoots. "It is a day of poetry, of cosmic stillness," he informed us. "She is the Madonna agrarianistically developed."

When I noted, unobtrusively, that it was now two-thirty, he advised: "There are lessons to be learned on a day like this. Let it not be rushed; let it be savored. It is a day composed on the celestial lyre. An event. We need only stop at the Blue Goose tavern, my dear Nick, and we will get to Mecca in good time.

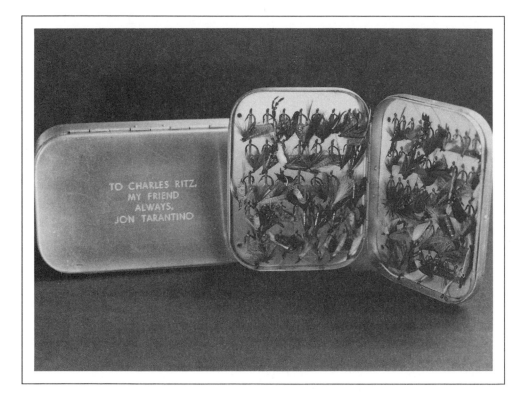

Branny, where is that oasis?"

Mike did not remember, but several inquiries proved that it was seven miles out of our way, up an unpaved road. No matter. It was impossible to fish the Beaverkill during the Green Drake hatch without first stopping at the Blue Goose. It was a ritual. Part of the sacraments. The Blue Goose was a holy place, a temple pilgrimages were made to.

It looked like a cruddy overaged bar to me. We stayed an hour, but only two miracles occurred: the floor rose three inches on my fourth beer, and I was able to walk out. We took a six-pack with us and were on our way, due west, over the last little mountains, pilgrim pioneers, seekers of the holy Mecca.

We arrived in Roscoe at five-thirty, still in time for a long evening's fishing, but Hawkes thought we should look up Bishop Harry Darbee before heading for the stream, to seek his blessings as well as his advice. This could not be done directly. It was first necessary to head for the Antrim Lodge, to the cool dark cellar for a few stronger snorts than we'd had. Hawkes invoked us each to empty two double shots of Jack Daniels, which done, he launched into a series of incisive questions of the good bartender. But when that dispenser of firewater said that the water had been high and that a few men had been in that very afternoon with limits they'd taken on spinning rods, Hawkes became violent and Brannigan had to grab his arm, even hold his mouth, as he shouted, "Coffee grinders! Hoodlums! Saracens!"

Darbee was not to be found, but Walt Dette was home, and Hawkes conned him out of a dozen hackles from a natural blue, after an hour of talk about breeding of this rare bird.

At seven o'clock we hit the stream. Not ten miles downriver, where Dette had told us to go, but a spot directly below Junction Pool. One look at the water, after that interminable drive, and I had insisted. Hawkes shrugged. It did not make much difference, he said.

Once parked, Mike and I suited and set up hurriedly. Hawkes sat back and puffed at his pipe. "Long as you two have the Saint Vitus' Dance, you might as well indulge it. Go on. Git, you two. Takes an old man like me a while to get into the proper frame of mind for his holy stream. It is not to be rushed."

We wasted no time. Brannigan headed downstream, I up—and we were flailing away wildly at the waters for a full twenty minutes before Hawkes, on stiff legs, puffing contentedly on his pipe, ambled to the spot on the stream nearest the car. Fish were beginning to rise steadily just at that moment, and the large pale-green duns began to rise in swarms from the water. I switched from a Cahill to a #12 Pale Watery Dun, and then to a White Miller, a White Wulff, and then to an imitation Drake. All in rapid succession. Nothing. Something was missing. My mind was beerfogged, my casting was sloppy, I was wobbly, and something important was trying to press itself out of my unconscious. Below me, Brannigan, fishing nymphs dead drift, took nothing.

Hawkes waded out a few feet, stood stark still like a crane, fixed his glasses, took the temperature of the water, tested it with his hand, peered long into the swirling duns, the many dimples of rising fish, and selected a fly from his single aluminum case. It took him a full minute to affix it, but when he had he looked at the water again, clipped off the fly, and started the process again. He pulled the leader tight, clipped off the end bit, ran the leader through his mouth six or seven times, and peeled off line.

I was staggered when his first cast brought a strike only moments after the fly had alighted. Deftly he played an eleven-inch brown, drew it close until it turned belly up, and then neatly netted it.

The scene was unbelievable. The sun was several feet above the tree line now, and seemed to hang, luminous and diffused, ready to drop at any moment. The hatch was fantastic, the large pale green drakes thick as locusts, heavy-winged and fat. Lesiurely two- and even three-pound trout stalked them, inches beneath the surface. It was like a slow-motion film. They would cruise, like sharks, their dorsals extended above the water line, and heavily suck down the fallen drakes. Everything took place on the surface—methodically, devastatingly. There must have been fifty trout cruising in that long flat pool—no doubt, many were denizens of the large lakelike pool several hundred yards downstream. They were in no hurry. For them it was an event, an annual feast some of them had probably partaken of for four or five years. My hands and limbs were shaking.

Hawkes' next cast brought another strike, but it was short and he retrieved the line quietly, without a ruffle of the surface.

I made a full twelve casts before he cast again, and this time the rise to his fly—

which I could not see—was not short. While playing what was obviously a two-pound trout or better, he called softly for me to come to his position. I scampered through the water like a water buffalo, convinced that he had both the right spot and the right fly, and scurried to his side just as he netted a fine eighteen-inch brown, broke its neck, and creeled it.

I was frantic. There could not be more than another thirty-five minutes of visibility. Wildly I tried four or five different flies, my back cast slapping the water behind me noisily. Hawkes did not frown. He did not take his eyes from the water. I had never seen such intense concentration.

Then I remembered—*how could I have forgotten?*—and my entire body shook with excitement as I did: the Pigeon Drake.

I was so unhinged that it took five tries before I got the leader through the eye of this miraculous fly, and when I jerked the knot tight the line broke. I tried again and this time managed. The Pigeon Drake hung convincingly from my line.

Carefully I false-cast out fifteen, then twenty feet of line. I felt calm and confident now, as icy and knowledgeable and canny as Hawkes. Then I released the last few feet of line, shot them through the guides, and happily, expectantly, watched the fly drop to the water.

It landed like a shot pigeon. But immediately one of those slow-motion monsters glided portentously toward it. I watched, heart beating wildly, while the dorsal neared. The spotted back of the fine brown and each and every aspect of his awesome body were clear to me as he moved, inches below the surface. Then he stopped, the fly not four inches from his nose. The trout was motionless, but not tense. "Take it. Take it, you old soak," I whispered. I twitted the fly. "Take it," I murmured again. Once more I twitched the fly, and this time the movement did it. When the reverberations in the water ceased, the fly began to sink, like the City in the Sea, majestically down. Unmistakably, the trout turned its nose up. It did. I'll swear to it. And then, with noble calm it glided toward a nearby natural, and took it. It had been a sneer—the sophisticated sneer of a wiseacre trout if I'd ever seen one. And it finished me. Dejectedly I retrieved my line, clipped off the fly, dropped it into the water (where it promptly sank like a stone), reeled in my line, and dismantled my rod.

In the remaining half hour of visibility Hawkes calmly took three more fish, the largest a full twenty inches, minutes before darkness set in.

The drive home, after Hawkes had finished three almost raw hamburgers and two cups of black coffee, took exactly sixty-two minutes. Hawkes did not particularly race along the road.

All the way back I had visions of those swarms of greenish duns rising from the flat pool, fluttering clumsily, falling back, drifting downstream, and being leisurely sharked down by slow-motion monsters. Brannigan had caught nothing; I had caught nothing; three anglers we met had taken one small trout among them; innumerable trout fishers throughout the East take nothing during the massive Green Drake hatches; but Hawkes had taken six in about an hour, using no more than several dozen casts. Alas, I can only further the myth about Hawkes: I certainly cannot disprove it.

He evaded all our questions for the first forty-five minutes of that quick drive home with a skill to dwarf Falstaff's.

"Yes, it did seem like the Green Drake, *Ephemera guttulata Pictet,* was the major hatch."

"You're not saying they weren't taking those duns, are you?" asked Mike pointedly. "I saw them take a dozen myself."

"Exactly what were you using?" I asked.

"How, how, how! An extraordinary question. Not at all an easy question to answer, my dear Nick. There are a dozen subtle factors involved that . . . "

"Come off it, Hawkes," said Brannigan.

". . . that the unenlightened Irishmen who slash the streams—and whom it has been my misfortune to fall in with during my decline—would scarcely understand. Brannigan, Branny old boy, did you see the innocence, the absolute simplicity of that farmgirl holding her child this afternoon? The Madonna—no less."

"Will you simply tell us what fly you were using?" Mike persisted.

"A question impossible to answer, beyond my power to answer. Ah, but did you see the colors of the sun settling below the tree line, the ochers, the magentas, the great song of the heavens? You must scatter my ashes there, Branny. It is so written."

We were silent while he dropped us off at Brannigan's house, carefully unloading all our tackle—this time without comment. He asked if we'd like a fish apiece (though not the two trophies).

We both said no.

Then he got back into his car stiffly, turned over the motor, looked at us both with those ancient and shadowy eyes, smiled, and said: "It was an event, gentlemen—was it not? We have been to Mecca. And it will last longer than these six trout, which I shall dispatch shortly—the least part of our trip."

"You won't tell us what you took them on?" I asked.

"You've missed the point. Nick," he said, taking my hand in his bony fingers, "until next year . . ."

With that he drove off around Brannigan's graveled circle and up the road. We could see the old Dodge pause on the highway. Hawkes leaned far out of the car, looked up at the moon, and said something loudly that we could not hear.

"Perhaps it *will* last longer," said Mike, putting his arm around my shoulder and smiling broadly there in the moonlight. I started preparing for the long trip back to the city, for the long year.

"Perhaps," I said.

And it has.

Tuna Fishing in Spain

Ernest Hemingway

Written in his early twenties, as a news dispatch, this short piece on the tuna of Vigo Bay prefigures a lot of later Hemingway, in books like The Sun Also Rises *and* The Old Man and the Sea *and in many stories: the abiding love of sport, the shrewd eye for detail when on or near water, the "purification" that comes from an honorable struggle. Only the adjectives will have to be thinned out.*
—NL

The Toronto Star Weekly
February 18, 1922

Vigo, Spain.—Vigo is a pasteboard-looking village, cobble-streeted, white- and orange-plastered, set up on one side of a big, almost landlocked harbor that is large enough to hold the entire British navy. Sun-baked brown mountains slump down to the sea like tired old dinosaurs, and the color of the water is as blue as a chrome of the bay at Naples.

A gray pasteboard church with twin towers and a flat, sullen fort that tops the hill where the town is set up look out on the blue bay, where the good fishermen will go when snow drifts along the northern streams and trout lie nose to nose in deep pools under a scum of ice. For the bright, blue chrome of a bay is alive with fish.

It holds schools of strange, flat, rainbow-colored fish, hunting-packs of long, narrow Spanish mackerel, and big, heavy-shouldered sea bass with odd, soft-sounding names. But principally it holds the king of all fish, the ruler of the Valhalla of fishermen.

The fisherman goes out on the bay in a brown lateen-sailed boat that lists drunkenly and determinedly and sails with a skimming pull. He baits with a silvery sort of a mullet and lets his line out to troll. As the boat moves along, there is a silver splatter in the sea as though a bushel full of buckshot had been tossed in. It is a school of sardines jumping out of the water, forced out by the swell of a big tuna who breaks water with a boiling crash and shoots his entire length of six feet into the air. It is then that the fisherman's heart lodges against his palate, to sink to his heels when the tuna falls back into the water with the noise of a horse diving off a dock.

A big tuna is silver and slate-blue, and when he shoots up into the air from close beside the boat it is like a blinding fish of quicksilver. He may weigh three hundred pounds and he jumps with the eagerness and ferocity of a mammoth rainbow trout. Sometimes five and six tuna will be in the air at once in Vigo Bay, shouldering out of the water like porpoises as they herd the sardines, then leaping in a towering jump that is as clean and beautiful as the first leap of a well-hooked rainbow.

The Spanish boatmen will take you out to fish for them for a dollar a day. There are plenty of tuna and they take the bait. It is a back-sickening, sinew-straining, man-sized job even with a rod that looks like a hoe handle. But if you land a big tuna after a six-hour fight, fight him man against fish until your muscles are nauseated with the unceasing strain, and finally bring him up alongside the boat, green-blue and silver in the lazy ocean, you will be purified and will be able to enter unabashed into the presence of the very elder gods and they will make you welcome.

Few poets have taken either the sport of fishing or its quarry to the level of art. John Engels has, and so has Ted Hughes; Heaney's "Trout"—with its undercurrent of gun and force imagery, played against the lithe and delicate movement of a fish that can slip "like butter down/the throat of the river"—is one of the very best.

—NL

Trout

Seamus Heaney

Hangs, a fat gun-barrel,
deep under arched bridges
or slips like butter down
the throat of the river.

From depths smooth-skinned as plums
his muzzle gets bull's eye;
picks off grass-seed and moths
that vanish, torpedoed.

Where water unravels
over gravel-beds he
is fired from the shallows
white belly reporting

flat; darts like a tracer-
bullet back between stones
and is never burnt out.
A volley of cold blood

ramrodding the current.

The Long Light

Le Anne Schreiber

This magical memoir records a voyage away from cities to the country, and thence to rivers and trout and fly fishing. In it, the move leads a daughter to a growing connection to her father and what he loves—a connection that slips past death.
—NL

41

I was born craving summer, not for its warmth or colors or breezes. From the womb, I wanted light, as much of it as my freshly opened eyes could withstand. Since I was born in early August, I was born satisfied, or at least I would like to think so. But that first dark November, and every one since then, came as a blow.

It's not that summer light is more beautiful than any other season's; it's just that there's more of it, and, make no mistake, when it comes to light, more is better; ask any Scandinavian; ask any sufferer of seasonally adjusted depression; ask me.

Being outdoors on a sunlit day is the only self-justifying state of existence I know; it follows that being indoors on sunlit days requires a lot of explaining, and what explanations I have been able to provide never suffice. I was born knowing this, as I say, but it took me forty Novembers to arrange my life around the knowledge. Lacking independent wealth or the skills of a forest ranger (they spend too much time in the shade anyway), it took some doing.

The ten years I spent working in high-pay, low-light jobs helped, especially the thirty months I toiled in the windowless precincts of a newspaper sports department. After long fluorescent days, I was too depressed, too without desire, to spend the money I earned. So I toiled in darkness, saving for a sunny day.

On the brink of forty, single and self-propelled, I left offices behind. I climbed my way out from under the rock of Manhattan and moved to Ancram, New York. There I quickly discovered that getting in the vicinity of light isn't enough. You still have to figure out how to let it fall on you, which is not as easy as it sounds.

There is simple basking, which has a lot to be said for it, but most of us lack the sublime temperament for prolonged, purposeless delight. It's the price we pay for not being lizards. There's sun bathing, which is just a hazardous form of napping, or one can simply do outdoors the things one routinely does indoors, like reading and dining. The trouble is, doing outdoors what one might better do indoors just leads to an indoor frame of mind. Who needs those page-flapping breezes anyway?

Which brings me to fishing. I was resistant at first. I remembered summer vacations as a child, fishing with my father in a tippy aluminum rowboat on a lake in Wisconsin, snagging weeds and getting sunburned. We were after plump, tasty bass, but the usual reward for long periods of strictly enforced silence, broken only by an occasional racket of squeaky oarlocks, was the sight of a lean, mean, ugly, oily, snaggle-toothed fish called northern pike.

So when my tackle-bearing father visited me for Thanksgiving that first country fall, I politely thanked him for the hand-me-down rods and spared him my memories. Since legal fishing season was months away, there was no immediate need to confess my utter lack of interest. I looked attentive as he demonstrated his fly-casting skills in my snow-crusted backyard and kept up pretenses by showing him my favorite spot on the stream whose steep bank formed the back border of my property.

In my early searches for idyllic basking sites, I had discovered a fallen sycamore whose double trunk spanned the stream from bank to bank, offering itself first as a cradle for my early, failed attempts at basking, later as seat and footrest for my contemplation of that failure.

One light-filled afternoon, while pondering the difference between humans and lizards, I noticed a flash of silver in the water, which marked the beginning of my life as a fish watcher. Nearly every day since then I had spent an hour or two sitting on my perch staring into the water, watching dark shadows dart across the streambed at my approach and then slowly slink back as the creatures that cast them realized it was just the lady without a pole.

By Thanksgiving, we had reached the point in our relationship where I could intentionally cast a shadow over their backs and they wouldn't bother to stir. Hooks were out of the question, I thought, as my father and I sidestepped together across the frosty log to the center of the stream. "Trout," he said, gazing into the swirling water with a wide smile of anticipation.

I had planned to keep my vigil on the sycamore all through the winter, not suspecting, of course, that within two weeks, the stream would be frozen solid from bank to bank. By Christmas, an opaque veil of ice stood between me and my fish, and nothing but spring could draw the veil back.

I waited. Those rods, stashed and forgotten in the rear of an upstairs closet, waited. Slowly, the afternoons began to lengthen. The ice thinned, turned transparent and finally succumbed to the swollen urgency of the stream rushing beneath it.

April came, and I resumed my perch on the sycamore log. May came, and I wanted to get into the water I was watching. What's the harm, I thought, in just pretending I'm fishing, strolling rod in hand through the sun-flicked stream, catching reflections. I could walk a stretch of the stream sufficiently distant from the sycamore that the fish gathered there would never have to see that suspicious long extension of my arm's shadow.

Some days I started downstream from the sycamore, at a shallow, fast-flowing stretch of the stream that suddenly stilled and deepened as it went round a bend and under a bridge. Other days I headed way upstream to a series of small falls and pools, always stopping well short of the sycamore.

Taking tips from neighborhood boys, I fished first with live bait minnows and worms. I was rewarded with nibbles, which seemed enough. I wasn't really fishing, after all, just playing a game of hide and seek with the trout, and I counted each quick tug as a tag. I was getting to know the stream, certain stretches of it inch by inch. My sneakered feet searched the rocky streambed for secure footings while my eyes scanned the surface for signals. I took my cues from light and its interruptions, from shadows cast by overhanging trees or passing clouds or birds flying overhead, the darkening of the water over a submerged boulder or a deep hole in the streambed. Standing in light, I cast into darknesses where a trout might rest—cool, still, hidden—waiting for a morsel to tempt him into movement.

Then I caught my first fish, not on live bait, but on a twirling three-hooked lure that embedded itself, irretrievably, two hooks up and one down, deep in the throat of a very young, inexperienced, pink-finned brook trout. I watched it gasp and flap in my hand, watched its shimmering vibrancy turn dull and listless, then still and blacken.

I had fallen in love with my light-filled game without ever believing it might come to this end. Nothing in my father's smile on the sycamore log that day contained a warning, nothing in my memory of our days on those Wisconsin lakes prepared me for this mangling. Catching, cleaning, eating, yes, but not this purposeless kill.

I called my father, and without blaming him outright for my sins, I let him know I wished he had never left those rods behind. He understood my distress but drew a different conclusion. The fault was not in fishing but in how one fished. For a different end, I needed a different means. I needed a fly rod, and if I would look in that closet again, I would see he left me two—"both real honeys," a fiberglass and an "old split bamboo."

He would tie me some flies on hooks too small to hurt the most newly spawned fish. I could remove them from a fish lip with a flick of the wrist and release a trout, no sadder but wiser, to the stream. Should the hook be embedded more deeply, he had just the thing—a scissor-handled surgical clamp, the kind doctors use to remove stitches from humans.

Within three days I was back in the stream, unencumbered by minnow bucket or worm can or tackle box full of lures. I traveled light now, just a few bits of string and feather wrapped around tiny hooks, stuck in sponge and stuffed in my vest pocket. And a whippy, near-weightless rod.

Since my goal now was to imitate what hovers just above the water, I raised my sights a notch, taking in the air and light as well as the water they stir and dapple. My focus lengthened, as did the summer afternoons, which now extended well into evening before I even considered leaving the stream.

To my father's and my amazement, I began to catch respectable sized trout almost immediately. With his help I mastered the art of quick release; the trick is patience, taking the time to play the fish out before reeling him in, so he arrives quietly in your hand, too tired to resist the flip of the wrist that will free him.

We were in league with the trout, allies in their progress from season to season, training them to fend off the harsher assaults of worm-danglers and hardware flingers. At the end of long days in the stream, I called my father with news of the catch: a ten-inch brookie, a twelve-inch brown, the sight of a great blue heron lifting off at my approach, an eight-point buck crossing the stream at the riffles, a sleekheaded muskrat diving for the cover of his underwater door in the bank.

I described whatever flitted above the stream, and he tied its likeness for me. Our phones seemed connected not by fiber optics but by the most delicately tapered of leaders, so sensitive that he felt the float of each fly, felt each slow swish of tail as the just-released trout steadied itself in the water before racing out of my loosely cupped hand.

He made my learning easy, but one thing I learned the hard way. "That's too bad," is all my father said when I told him I had broken the tip of my rod on a careless back cast into a tree branch. The next day, when I took the "old split bamboo" to the tackle shop for repair, I was unprepared for the whistles of appreciation and dismay that greeted the sight of my broken rod. In my ignorance, I had chosen it over the fiberglass as the best rod for a beginner to bumble with.

"Do you know what you've got here?" the shop owner asked, and I pretended that I had always known what I was just beginning to understand. He told me he knew a guy over in Massachusetts who used to repair split bamboo just for the love of it, but he might be out of business now, because hardly anybody who has a split bamboo rod actually fishes with it anymore. They just hold on to them as investments.

When I told my father the guy in Massachusetts thought the rod could be repaired but it would never be whippy again, he said, "Well, I've caught a lot of good fish on fiberglass." For the next three trout seasons, so did I.

The phone and mail flowed between us like the stream, rising to its highest level in late spring and tapering off to a trickle in the fall.

He sent me flies, and I sent him photographs of my favorite stretch of the stream; one time I even included a diagram showing the exact spots where I had seen the buck crossing, the heron lifting off, the big one that always gets away. Each year he planned a visit so we could enter the stream together, but each summer he was detained, first by my mother's illness, then by his own.

On my last visit to him, I saw that he kept those pictures at his bedside. Thumbworn at the corners, they still glistened at the center. One August morning, he asked if we could talk about a few things, "just in case." He said he would like a portion of his ashes to enter the stream, and I said I knew just where. No, not where the sycamore spanned the stream; the winter after my mother died, the sycamore had been pried loose from its mooring on the bank by the force of high water released during a rare January thaw. Without the fallen sycamore to slow and deepen the stream, there was nothing special to keep the fish there and they had departed.

There was a better spot now, I told him, and picking up a photograph, I pointed to the riffles where I had seen the buck highstep, head erect, across the stream and disappear into the woods. Anything that entered the stream there would flow downstream past all the spots marked on the diagram to the stretches I would explore next summer and the summer after that. He smiled at the idea, and that's all it was, an idea, "just in case."

Then he asked me to go down to the basement, to the workshop where he tied flies and fixed whatever was broken, because there were some things down there he wanted me to have some day.

His work table was in order, cleared of projects for the first time in my memory. Sitting on the table was the wicker creel I had seen in pictures of him fishing as a young man. I looked closely this time, saw the well-oiled leather of the creel's shoulder strap and harness, its polished silver clasps. Next to the creel was a long oak case that I had never seen before. I opened it and found five pristine sections of split bamboo rod, with three different end sections of varying weights and whippiness.

It is spring now. The afternoons are beginning to linger. Rod and creel and ashes wait with me for summer, for the long light, when they will enter the stream at the riffles. Sometimes I wonder if the creel is his permission for me to keep what I catch. Right now, it seems more important that he taught me how to release.

This summer I will carry the creel, empty, and bear the wicker weight of his absence. They say death comes as an invitation to light. I hope so. I would like to think of life as a progress from light to light.

Abe Lincoln Fished Here

Lin Sutherland

With a mother who is a "fishing fanatic" (despite a proper Charleston upbringing and seven daughters) anything can happen and often does—as in this delicious narrative about a marvelous trip from Austin to South Carolina when the author was ten. You may not fish with blood bait, but you'll forgive the great woman who does once you get to know her.
—NL

My mother was a fishing fanatic despite her Charleston, South Carolina, blue-blood upbringing. When she was twenty she graduated magna cum laude from the College of Charleston and left that city of history and suffocating social rules forever. With the twenty-dollar gold piece she got for the Math Prize, she bought a railroad ticket for as far west as it would get her. Austin, Texas, was $19.02 away.

There she met my father, a poet and horseman, and proceeded to have seven children—all girls. She also took up fishing, and by the time I was born, she had enough tackle, lawn chairs, and fishing hats to fill a steamer trunk. To my father's horror, her favorite lure was blood bait. Bass and catfish were her prey.

Every summer it was my mother's custom to pack the seven of us girls into the DeSoto and drive from Austin to Charleston to visit our grandparents. We camped and fished the whole way.

Mama's preparations for the fifteen hundred-mile trip consisted of packing the car with seven army cots, a basket of Stonewall peaches and sixteen gallons of live bait, with her tackle box and assorted rods and reels thrown in. Her idea of successful traveling was to get us all in the car without one of us sitting on the blood bait or being left at a gas station. Once she'd done a head count and ascertained the security of the bait, she'd drive like A. J. Foyt until it was too dark to go any farther. This meant we were usually tired, hungry, and lost on some back road in the middle of Louisiana or Mississippi when we stopped to camp.

"Stopping to camp" in our case meant suddenly swerving off the road when my mother spied a river or lake that stirred her sporting blood. She never once planned our stops like normal people do, timing themselves to arrive at a campsite or park around dusk. But this was the 1950s, when people still slept with the screen door unlocked and left the keys in the car. We felt perfectly safe at any roadside area, and we were.

The trip that brought us face to face with history was the one we took in the summer of 1958 when I was ten. It started normally enough. We had driven all day from Austin, into the dark and the Deep South. From the back seat, groggy and weary from the hours of travel, my sisters and I felt our mother wheel the car onto the shoulder and turn off the motor.

In the dim glow of our flashlights, we pulled out the army cots, set them up and sucked on leftover peach pits. We wanted to drop into a dead sleep, but as far as Mama was concerned, this was a perfect time to go fishing.

The problem was, Mama never seemed to notice that she was the only one who ever caught anything bigger than a deck of cards. She also failed to recognize that she had borne seven girls, not seven Captain Ahabs. She lived under the illusion that everyone had the same enthusiasm as she did for sitting on rocks at waterside and waiting hours for something to steal the bait. Which of course never happened to her.

While we slouched around the camp making unintelligible grumbling noises, she unloaded the gallons of blood bait and her tackle box and got to work.

"Look at that big dark pool just under those cypress knees, honey," she said. "You just know there's a ten-pound bass waiting for me in there! I hope it's a stupid one." She whistled a snatch of "High Noon" as she explored her stock of lures, jigs and spoons.

Mama was very Zen about her fishing, giving it her complete concentration and ritualized observation. She examined each item in the tackle box with pleasure, murmuring to herself. She emerged from this reverie only when she decided on the right lure to use.

This night she announced, "I think I'll use my Good Luck Lure Number 242 on this baby." She glanced in my direction to see if I was watching and abruptly emitted a theatrical, diabolical laugh.

"He'll never escape my Magic Lucky Lure!" she went on. "We have ways of making fish welcome here at our little fish camp . . . no, Herr Lucky Lure?" Then, adjusting her fishing hat, she addressed the water in a tough-guy voice: "Prepare to meet your Maker, Lord Bass-ship."

And she cast perfectly into the heart of the cypress-root pool.

For her children, the enthusiasm and high drama my mother created around fishing was more intriguing than the activity itself. She was ceaselessly energetic and entertaining, and when she went up against a largemouth bass with a brain the size and density of a dust mote, it was no contest.

Fifteen minutes later she was addressing the bass in person as she cleaned it.

"I regret to inform you, Lord Bass-ship, that the inscrutable order of the universe has destined you to serve in the dual role of Main Guest and Dish at this

51

evening's festivities. You have my deepest sympathy. On the other hand, the jig's up for everybody at one time or another, Bud. Fire up the logs, girls. Dinner just arrived."

Our second day on the road we passed trees dripping with Spanish moss, stately old homes and vast fields of cotton and snap beans. We sang and talked and Mama told fish stories. And finally, in the pitch black somewhere deep into Mississippi, she stopped the car.

"I hear running water," she announced.

We bailed out of the DeSoto and traipsed down from the road until we found a place where the ground got gravelly. We figured we were far enough from the road so we wouldn't be run over in the middle of the night, and we set up our cots in the usual manner: jammed against each other in line, so that if, during the night, one of us flopped an arm or leg out, the warm body of a sister would be felt. Sitting cross-legged on the cots, we munched Vienna sausage and Wonderbread sandwiches and watched Mama fish in the fast-running creek next to us. Then we fell asleep, exhausted.

As the dawn light began to come up, something like a gentle lapping at my side awoke me. I slowly let a foot slide over the edge of my cot. It fell into two feet of cold water. I bolted upright and saw that seven sisters and their mother were about to float away.

My mother had camped us in a creekbed. The water had risen during the night from rains upstream and had us surrounded. We practically had to swim to the car, pulling our cots behind us.

The third night found us somewhere in the mountains of Kentucky. I was never quite sure where we were at any given point on these trips, since I knew only one landmark—the tree-lined road to my grandparents' house—the finish line. But again, we had driven for hours into the night futilely looking for water. When we finally pulled off the road, the hills around us were black as midnight under a skillet. Then a slice of a quarter moon slid out from behind a cloud and delicately illuminated a rock gate in front of us.

"Oh, look!" Mama cried, "a national park."

There was an audible sigh of relief from the back seat. "Let's camp here, Mama!" we clamored urgently.

Since she had been slapping her cheeks for the last hour to stay awake, she agreed.

We cruised down a black dirt road into the parking area. Nestled nearby was the outline of a log cabin. Beyond that, the glint of water.

"See that!" Mama said excitedly. "A sleeping cabin. By some kind of lake. This is paradise."

We parked and unloaded the car, dragging our stuff into the log cabin.

It was open and empty. We could see it was very old and rudimentary, but it had a bathroom with running water. For us it was luxury quarters. We bathed and ate our dinner of kipper snacks and soda crackers, with Moon Pies for dessert. Then we snuggled into the cots that we'd fixed up in the one bare room.

Mama set off with long strides toward the water, gear in hand. The faint murmur of her voice as she conversed with her tackle box drifted through the open windows. With that and a cozy roof overhead, my sisters curled up and fell to sleep like a litter of puppies.

I picked up my rod and reel and, still in my pajamas, slipped quietly out the door. Across the damp grass I could see my mother's silhouette making casting motions. For a moment I felt the thrill of anticipation inherent in fishing: there was a fat catfish with my name waiting out there, I just knew it.

I joined my mother and we fished together. Just us, the water and the quarter moon. It was one of those moments that form a permanent part in the book of parent-child memories, though it was destined to be brief. Mama could practically conjure fish up to her, and sure enough, within half an hour she got a strike and brought in a fourteen-pound cat. Probably *my* Fat-Cat, I thought irritably.

"Look," she said, bending around me, her hands grasping mine as I held my rod. "Let me show you . . . " She made a deft flicking motion and suddenly my line shot across the water. The light of the moon made it look like the trail of a shooting star. It fell silently on the dark water and disappeared. "Right *there*," she said lowly. "Hold tight to it."

She turned away and began cleaning her fish. I gripped the rod until my tiny knuckles were white. I had a feeling for what was coming. Suddenly, the line lurched tight and my arms shot forward. I almost flew into the black water of the lake.

"It's a big one, Mama!" I yelled. "I don't think I can hold it." My feet were slipping down the bank, and the mud had oozed up to my ankles. "Mama, quick!"

She grasped me around the waist and yanked me back up the bank. The pull on the line lessened. "Now! Bring it in now!" she shouted. I reeled in as hard as I could. Suddenly the fish was right there below me, lying in shallow water. It was a big one, all right. Almost as big as Mama's.

"Good work," she said, leaning over and carefully pulling the catfish onto the bank. It slapped the wet grass angrily. I was exhausted. We took our fish back to the cabin and fell into a deep sleep.

It seemed only minutes later that sleep was penetrated by voices. Lots of voices. Suddenly, the door of the cabin burst open and sunlight and a large group of people led by a woman in a uniform flowed into the room. The uniformed person was in the middle of a speech. "And here we have the boyhood home of President Abraham Lincoln—Aagghhhh!!"

We all screamed at once. My mother, protective in her own quixotic way, leapt off the cot, her chenille bathrobe flapping, and shouted at the intruders, "Who do you think you are, bursting in on a sleeping family like this?"

The guide was struck speechless. She gathered herself with visible effort. "Ma'am, I don't know who you are, but this is Abraham Lincoln's Birthplace National Historic Park," she reported tersely. Her eyes quickly shifted sideways to take in two huge catfish lying on the floor. Though she tried to conceal it, her lips pursed with disgust. I knew right off she wasn't a fisherman.

"And his log cabin," she continued, "is *not* an overnight stopover for fishing expeditions. This is a restricted area with guided tours beginning at 7 A.M. and . . ."

"Oh my God, we overslept!" Mama shouted. "Pack the car, girls. We've got to get on the road!"

We lurched into a flurry of experienced cot-folding and were out the door in seconds.

"But, ma'am," the guide called at my mother's disappearing back, "You weren't supposed to sleep in here. This is Lincoln's Log Cabin. *It's a National*

Treasure!"

"We treasure our night here," my mother shouted back, as she gunned the car around. "Abe wouldn't have minded."

With that we roared off in the direction of South Carolina. I saw a sign as we left: Leaving Hodgenville, Kentucky, Abraham Lincoln's Birthplace. Ya'll Come Back.

"Not likely," my mother laughed. "A good fishing spot, but I hate to do anything twice, don't you?"

And that's how it happened that, during the summer I was ten, the course of history was changed. Unofficially, to be sure, but if there'd been a historical marker by that lake, it would now have to read Abe Lincoln Fished Here . . . And So Did I.

Mr. Theodore Castwell

G. E. M. Skues

We all long for halcyon days, when trout come to our every cast,
and at first Mr. Theodore Castwell is ecstatic about his excellent sport—as we'd all be.
I think I really understood this story when I taught Plato's "Apology" and
a student said he thought talking to Odysseus and Homer for an eternity was madness;
he'd rather hit golf balls.
—NL

Mr. Theodore Castwell, having devoted a long, strenuous and not unenjoyable life to hunting to their doom innumerable salmon, trout, and grayling in many quarters of the globe, and having gained much credit among his fellows for his many ingenious improvements in rods, flies, and tackle employed for that end, in the fullness of time died and was taken to his own place.

St. Peter looked up from a draft balance sheet at the entry of the attendant angel.

"A gentleman giving the name of Castwell. Says he is a fisherman, your Holiness, and has 'Fly-Fishers' Club, London' on his card."

"Hm-hm," says St. Peter. "Fetch me the ledger with his account."

St. Peter perused it.

"Hm-hm," said St. Peter. "Show him in."

Mr. Castwell entered cheerfully and offered a cordial right hand to St. Peter.

"As a brother of the angle—" he began.

"Hm-hm," said St. Peter. "I have been looking at your account from below."

"I am sure I shall not appeal to you in vain for special consideration in connection with the quarters to be assigned to me here."

"Hm-hm," said St. Peter.

"Well, I've seen worse accounts," said St. Peter. "What sort of quarters would you like?"

"Do you think you could manage something in the way of a country cottage of the Test Valley type, with modern conveniences and, say, three quarters of a mile of one of those pleasant chalk streams, clear as crystal, which proceed from out the throne, attached?"

"Why, yes," said St. Peter. "I think we can manage that for you. Then what about your gear? You must have left your fly rods and tackle down below. I see you prefer a light split cane of nine foot or so, with appropriate fittings. I will indent upon the Works Department for what you require, including a supply of flies. I think you will approve of our dresser's productions. Then you will want a keeper to attend you."

"Thanks awfully, your Holiness," said Mr. Castwell. "That will be first-rate. To tell you the truth, from the Revelations I read, I was inclined to fear that I might be just a teeny-weeny bit bored in heaven."

"In h-hm-hm," said St. Peter, checking himself.

It was not long before Mr. Castwell found himself alongside an enchantingly beautiful clear chalk stream, some fifteen yards wide, swarming with fine trout feeding greedily: and presently the attendant angel assigned to him had handed him the daintiest, most exquisite, light split-cane rod conceivable—perfectly balanced with the reel and line—with a beautifully damped tapered cast of incredible fineness and strength, and a box of flies of such marvelous tying as to be almost mistakable for the natural insects they were to simulate.

Mr. Castwell scooped up a natural fly from the water, matched it perfectly from the fly box, and knelt down to cast to a riser putting up just under a tussock ten yards or so above him. The fly lit like gossamer, six inches above the last ring; and next moment the rod was making the curve of beauty. Presently, after an exciting battle, the keeper netted out a beauty of about two and a half pounds.

"Heavens," cried Mr. Castwell. "This is something like."

"I am sure his Holiness will be pleased to hear it," said the keeper.

Mr. Castwell prepared to move upstream to the next riser when he noticed that another trout had taken up the position of that which he had just landed, and was rising. "Just look at that," he said, dropping instantaneously to his knee and drawing off some line. A moment later an accurate fly fell just above the neb of the fish, and instantly Mr. Castwell engaged in battle with another lusty fish. All went well, and presently the landing net received its two and a half pounds.

"A very pretty brace," said Mr. Castwell, preparing to move on to the next string of busy nebs which he had observed putting up around the bend. As he approached the tussock, however, he became aware that the place from which he had just extracted so satisfactory a brace was already occupied by another busy feeder.

"Well, I'm damned," said Mr. Castwell. "Do you see that?"

"Yes, sir," said the keeper.

The chance of extracting three successive trout from the same spot was too attractive to be forgone, and once more Mr. Castwell knelt down and delivered a perfect cast to the spot. Instantly it was accepted and battle was joined. All held, and presently a third gleaming trout joined his brethren in the creel.

Mr. Castwell turned joyfully to approach the next riser round the bend. Judge,

however, his surprise to find that once more the pit beneath the tussock was occupied by a rising trout, apparently of much the same size as others.

"Heavens," exclaimed Mr. Castwell. "Was there ever anything like it?"

"No, sir," said the keeper.

"Look here," said he to the keeper, "I think I really must give this chap a miss and pass on to the next."

"Sorry, it can't be done, sir. His Holiness would not like it."

"Well, if that's really so," said Mr. Castwell, and knelt rather reluctantly to his task.

Several hours later he was still casting to the same tussock.

"How long is this confounded rise going to last?" inquired Mr. Castwell. "I suppose it will stop soon."

"No, sir," said the keeper.

"What, isn't there a slack hour in the afternoon?"

"No afternoon, sir."

"What? Then what about the evening rise?"

"No evening rise, sir," said the keeper.

"Well, I shall knock off now. I must have had about thirty brace from that-corner."

"Beg pardon, sir, but his Holiness would not like that."

"What?" said Mr. Castwell. "Mayn't I even stop at night?"

"No night here, sir," said the keeper.

"Then do you mean that I have got to go on catching these damned two-and-a-half pounders at this corner forever and ever?"

The keeper nodded.

"Hell!" said Mr. Castwell.

"Yes," said his keeper.

Murder

Sparse Grey Hackle

*All obsessive fly fisherman are different, but they all overlap.
John's fight with a great trout in "Murder" is one of the memorable representations of such
a battle in angling literature—and earns its worthy resolution.*
—NL

I f fishing interferes with your business, give up your business," any angler will tell you, citing instances of men who have lost health and even life through failure to take a little recreation, and reminding you that "the trout do not rise in Greenwood Cemetery," so you had better do your fishing while you are still able. But you will search far to find a fisherman to admit that a taste for fishing, like a taste for liquor, must be governed lest it come to possess its possessor; that an excess of fishing can cause as many tragedies of lost purpose, earning power, and position as an excess of liquor. This is the story of a man who finally decided between his business and his fishing, and of how his decision was brought about by the murder of a trout.

Fishing was not a pastime with my friend John but an obsession—a common condition, for typically your successful fisherman is not really enjoying a recreation, but rather taking refuge from the realities of life in an absorbing fantasy in which he grimly if subconsciously reenacts in miniature the unceasing struggle of primitive man for existence. Indeed, it is that which makes him successful, for it gives him that last measure of fierce concentration, that final moment of unyielding patience which in angling so often make the difference between fish and no fish.

John was that kind of fisherman, more so than any other I ever knew. Waking or sleeping, his mind ran constantly on the trout and its taking, and back in 1932 I often wondered whether he could keep on indefinitely doing business with the surface of his mind and fishing with the rest of his mental processes—wondered, and feared that he could not. So when he called me one spring day and said, "I'm tired of sitting here and watching a corporation die; let's go fishing," I know that he was not discouraged with his business so much as he was impatient with its restraint. But I went with him, for maybe I'm a bit obsessed myself.

That day together on the river was like a thousand other pages from the book of any angler's memories. There was the clasp and pull of cold, hurrying water on our legs, the hours of rhythmic casting, and the steady somnambulistic shuffling which characterizes steel workers aloft and fly fishermen in fast water. Occasionally our heads were bent together over a fly box; at intervals our pipes wreathed smoke, and from time to time a brief remark broke the silence. We were fishing "pool and pool" together, each as he finished walking around the other to a new spot above him.

Late afternoon found me in the second pool below the dam, throwing a long line up the still water. There was a fish rising to some insect so small that I could not detect it, so I was using a tiny gray fly on a long leader with a 5X point. John came by and went up to the dam pool and I lost interest in my refractory fish and walked up to watch, for there was always a chance of a good fish there. I stopped at a safe distance and sat down on a rock with my leader trailing to keep it wet, while John systematically covered the tail of the pool until he was satisfied that there were no fish there to dart ahead and give the alarm, and then stepped into it.

As he did so his body became tense, his posture that of a man who stalks his enemy. With aching slowness and infinite craft he began to inch up the pool and as he went his knees bent more and more until he was crouching. Finally, with his rod low to the water and one hand supporting himself on the bottom of the stream, he crept to a casting position and knelt in mid-current with water lapping under his elbows, his left sleeve dripping unheeded as he allowed the current to straighten his line behind him. I saw that he was using the same leader as mine but with a large No. 12 fly.

"John, using 5X?" I breathed. Without turning his head he nodded almost imperceptibly.

"Better break off and reknot," I counseled softly, but he ignored the suggestion. I spoke from experience. Drawn 5X gut is almost as fine as a human hair, and we both knew that it chafes easily where it is tied to a fly as heavy as No. 12, so that it is necessary to make the fastening in a different spot at frequent intervals in order to avoid breaking it.

I kept silence and watched John. With his rod almost parallel to the water he picked up his fly from behind him with a light twitch and then false-cast to dry it. He was a good caster; it neither touched the surface nor rose far above it as he whipped it back and forth.

Now he began lengthening his line until finally, at the end of each forward cast, his fly hovered for an instant above a miniature eddy between the main current and a hand's breadth of still water which clung to the bank. And then I noticed what he had seen when he entered the pool—the sudden slight dimple denoting the feeding of a big fish on the surface.

The line came back with a subtle change from the wide-sweeping false casts, straightened with decision and swept forward in a tight roll. It straightened again and then checked suddenly. The fly swept round as a little elbow formed in the leader, and settled on the rim of the eddy with a loop of slack upstream of it. It started to circle, then disappeared in a sudden dimple and I could hear a faint sucking sound.

It seemed as if John would never strike although his pause must have been but momentary. Then his long line tightened—he had out fifty feet—as he drew it back with his left hand and gently raised the rod tip with his right. There was slight pause and then the line began to run out slowly.

Rigid as a statue, with the water piling a little wave against the brown waders at his waist, he continued to kneel there while the yellow line slid almost unchecked through his left hand. His lips moved.

"A big one," he murmured. "The leader will never hold him if he gets started. I should have changed it."

The tip of the upright rod remained slightly bent as the fish moved into the circling currents created by the spillway at the right side of the dam. John took line gently and the rod maintained its bend. Now the fish was under the spillway and must have dived down with the descending stream, for I saw a couple of feet of line slide suddenly through John's hand. The circling water got its impetus here and this was naturally the fastest part of the eddy.

The fish came rapidly toward us, riding with the quickened water, and John retrieved line. Would the fish follow the current around again, or would it leave it and run down past us? The resilient rod tip straightened as the pressure was eased. The big trout passed along the downstream edge of the eddy and swung over the bank to follow it round again, repeated its performance at the spillway, and again refused to leave the eddy. It was troubled and perplexed by the strange hampering of its progress but it was not alarmed, for it was not aware of our presence or even of the fact that it was hooked, and the restraint on it had not been enough to arouse its full resistance.

Every experienced angler will understand that last statement. The pull of a game fish, up to the full limit of its strength, seems to be in proportion to the resistance which it encounters. As I watched the leader slowly cutting the water, I recalled that often I had hooked a trout and immediately given slack, whereupon invariably it had moved quietly and aimlessly about, soon coming to rest as if it had no realization that it was hooked.

I realized now that John intended to get the "fight" out of his fish at a rate slow enough not to endanger his leader. His task was to keep from arousing the fish to a resistance greater than the presumably weakened 5X gut would withstand. It seemed as if it were hopeless, for the big trout continued to circle the eddy, swimming deep and strongly against the rod's light tension, which relaxed only when the fish passed the gateway of the stream below. Around and around it went, and then at last it left the eddy. Yet it did not dart into the outflowing current but headed into deep water close to the far bank. I held my breath, for over there was a tangle of roots, and I could imagine what a labyrinth they must make under the surface. Ah, it was moving toward the roots! Now what would John do—hold the fish hard and break off; check it and arouse its fury; or perhaps splash a stone in front of it to turn it back?

He did none of these but instead slackened off until his line sagged in a catenary curve. The fish kept on, and I could see the leader draw on the surface as it swam into the mass of roots. Now John dropped his rod flat to the water and delicately drew on the line until the tip barely flexed, moving it almost imperceptibly several times to feel whether his leader had fouled on a root. Then he lapsed into immobility.

I glanced at my wrist watch, slowly bent my head until I could light my cold pipe without raising my hand, and then relaxed on my rock. The smoke drifted lazily upstream, the separate puffs merging into a thin haze which dissipated itself imperceptibly. A bird moved on the bank. But the only really living thing was the stream, which rippled a bit as it divided around John's body and continually moved a loop of his yellow line in the disturbed current below him.

When the trout finally swam quietly back out of the roots, my watch showed that it had been there almost an hour and a quarter. John slackened the line and released a breath which he seemed to have been holding all that while, and the fish re-entered the eddy to resume its interminable circling. The sun, which had been in my face, dropped behind a tree, and I noted how the shadows had lengthened. Then the big fish showed itself for the first time, its huge dorsal fin appearing as it rose toward the surface and the lobe of its great tail as it turned down again; it seemed to be two feet long.

Again its tail swirled under the surface, puddling the water as it swam slowly and deliberately, and then I thought that we would lose the fish, for as it came around to the downstream side of the eddy it wallowed an instant and then headed toward us. Instantly John relaxed the rod until the line hung limp and from the side of his mouth he hissed, "Steady!"

Down the stream, passing John so closely that he could have hit it with his tip, drifted a long dark bulk, oaring along deliberately with its powerful tail in the smooth current. I could see the gray fly in the corner of its mouth and the leader hanging in a curve under its belly, then the yellow line floating behind. In a moment he felt of the fish again, determined that it was no longer moving, and resumed his light pressure, causing it to swim around aimlessly in the still water below us. The sun was half below the horizon now and the shadows slanting down over the river covered us. In the cool, diffused light the lines on John's face from nostril to mouth were deeply cut and the crafty folds at the outer corners of his lids hooded his eyes. His rod hand shook with a fine tremor.

The fish broke, wallowing, but John instantly dropped his rod flat to the water and slipped a little line. The fish wallowed again, then swam more slowly in a large circle. It was moving just under the surface now, its mouth open and its back breaking water every few feet, and it seemed to be half turned on its side. Still John did not move except for the small gestures of taking or giving line, raising or lowering his tip.

It was in the ruddy afterglow that the fish finally came to the top, beating its tail in a subdued rhythm. Bent double, I crept ashore and then ran through the brush to the edge of the still water downstream of the fish, which now was broad on its side. Stretching myself prone on the bank, I extended my net at arm's length and held it flat on the bottom in a foot of water.

John began to slip out line slowly, the now beaten trout moving feebly as the slow current carried it down. Now it was opposite me and I nodded a signal to John. He moved his tip toward my bank and cautiously checked the line. The current swung the trout toward me and it passed over my net.

I raised the rim quietly and slowly, and the next instant the trout was doubled up in my deep-bellied net and I was holding the top shut with both hands while the fish, galvanized into a furious flurry, splashed water in my face as I strove to get my feet under me.

John picked his way slowly down the still-water, reeling up as he came, stumbling and slipping on the stones like an utterly weary man. I killed the trout with my pliers and laid it on the grass as he came up beside me and stood watching it with bent head and sagging shoulders for a long while.

"To die like that!" he said as if thinking aloud. "Murdered—nagged to death; he never knew he was fighting for his life until he was in the net. He had strength and courage enough to beat the pair of us but we robbed him a little at a time until we got him where we wanted him. And then knocked him on the head. I wish you had let him go."

The twilight fishing, our favorite time, was upon us but he started for the car and I did not demur. We began to take off our wet shoes and waders.

"That's just what this depression is doing to me!" John burst out suddenly as he struggled with a shoelace. "Niggling me to death! And I'm up here fishing, taking two days off in the middle of the week, instead of doing something about it. Come on; hurry up. I'm going to catch the midnight to Pittsburgh; I know where I can get a contract."

And sure enough he did.

The Brakes Got Drunk

Red Smith

Red Smith, writing on any of a dozen sports, is a wonder—brilliant, irreverent, full of shrewd analogies and surprise. Trout suggest Tony Galento, Primo Carnero, and Jane Russell; a truck gassed with Vat 69 is not the best truck in Chile but surely the happiest; one person on the trip catches fish, the author catches backlashes and weeds. If you haven't read Red Smith on fishing, you're in for a great treat.

—NL

Laguna Del Maule, Chile, 1953

This typewriter is being beaten with fingers whose knuckles are bleeding and nails broken after hand-to-fin struggles with trout exactly the size, shape, and disposition of Tony Galento. Up here in the Andes fishing is a more perilous game than Russian roulette. If you survive the mountain road, there are rainbow in Lake Maule ready and willing to eat you for bait. Nothing is impossible to fish that live a mile and a half up in the sky.

Lake Maule perches on the Chilean-Argentine border about twenty kilometers and two thousand feet above the sparse grove of maytenus trees at timberline where camp had been pitched the evening before. The last drop of fluid had drained out of the brakes of the old Chevrolet truck during the journey to the campsite, and there are no filling stations along the narrow, twisting shelf that serves, more or less, as a road.

Herman, the driver, halted trucks that passed the camp occasionally with construction crews working on a dam at the lake. They told him oil would ruin the brakes, but said wine could serve as an emergency fluid.

"Because it contains alcohol, eh?" said Captain Warren Smith, of Panagra. "We can do better than that. Where's the Vat 69?"

The Chevrolet scrambled up to the lake with a boiling radiator and a full brake cylinder, not the best truck in Chile, but by all odds the happiest.

Maule straddles a pass in mountains entirely devoid of vegetation. They are bare peaks of volcanic rock crumbling into gray dust under the wind that blows eternally up this gorge from the west, making even these midsummer days uncomfortably cold. A little way out from the shore there is a belt of seaweed just under the surface where the trout lie and feed on a small pink crawfish called *pancora*. This shellfish diet gives the rainbows their majestic size, but it is the barren landscape that gives them their evil temperament. In all this desolation they brood.

Captain Smith and his North American burden rode by outboard to the east end of the lake, where snow touched the Chilean mountains rising from the water's edge and Argentine mountains showed just beyond. They started casting over the weed beds, using a smallish bronze-finish spoon of scarlet and orange. Almost immediately there was a grunt from the captain and a wild splash. Something dark and shiny and altogether implausible came out of the water and returned. It looked like a trout, but not like the sort of trout people ordinarily see when their eyes are open.

"You go on fishing," Captain Smith said. "I'll be awhile with this fellow."

His rod was a bow and his line hissed through the water. The fish was in and out of the lake, in and out, and then it was in the boat flopping on a gaff, a pink-striped brute of black and silver. "He'll hit about nine pounds," the captain said calmly.

Thereafter the captain caught fish and his companion caught backlashes and weeds. So intense, however, is the dislike these trout have for people that even the least proficient angler is bound to be under attack.

Between backlashes, a distant relative of Primo Carnera sprang up for a look at the latest New York styles in outdoor apparel, made a face of hideous disapproval, and spat out the spoon.

Another grabbed the same spoon and went into a terrifying rage.

Four times in quick succession he stood up on his tail, snarling and shaking his head and cursing horribly. On the fourth jump he snapped the leader.

Then Captain Smith had one that broke the leader and departed. Then it happened again to the amateur, but not before the whirling reel handle had smashed fingernails and stripped skin off awkward knuckles.

By now half the population of the lake had taken a passion for collecting hardware. Six leaders were snapped and six spoons confiscated by force before it was decided that the fifteen-pound test nylon was faulty. There's an awful lot of trout in Maule going around with their faces full of painted metal with nylon streamers. Maybe the style will catch on, like nose rings in the cannibal islands.

With the spoon tied directly to the casting line, anybody could catch fish. Practically anybody did. The outboard would take the boat upwind to the lee of a point or island; then the wind would drift it swiftly over the weed beds. Duck and geese and tern and grebe swam on the water. Except for one other fishing party, the place belonged to them and the fish.

"Let's take one more drift," the captain suggested, "and call it a day."

Half a moment later his companion screamed. The reel handle was snatched from his grasp and the drag sang. A trout leaped, fell back on his side. He looked six feet long. He dived, wrenching off line. The boat drifted on, but he wouldn't come along. Twice the captain ran the boat upwind, cautiously undoing knots the fish had tied around weeds. At length the sullen beast came aboard.

He was a good twelve pounds, broad-shouldered, magnificently colored, and splendidly deep, like Jane Russell.

Hairy Gertz and the Forty-Seven Crappies

Jean Shepherd

*Jean Shepherd is robust, wacky, hilarious, bursting with his own rare brand of vitality.
You'll never get a better dose of him than in this memorable account of how "the greatest
vicarious angler in the history of the Western world" fishes a muddy Northern Indiana
sump late one sweltering August night, at age twelve, with his father and a batch
of other men, and finally gets let into The Club . . . of adults.*
—NL

L ife, when you're a Male kid, is what the Grownups are doing. The Adult world seems to be some kind of secret society that has its own passwords, handclasps, and countersigns. The thing is to get In. But there's this invisible, impenetrable wall between you and all the great, unimaginably swinging things that they seem to be involved in. Occasionally mutterings of exotic secrets and incredible pleasures filter through. And so you bang against it, throw rocks at it, try to climb over it, burrow under it; but there it is. Impenetrable. Enigmatic.

Girls somehow seem to be already involved, as though from birth they've got the Word. Lolita has no Male counterpart. It does no good to protest and pretend otherwise. The fact is inescapable. A male kid is really a kid. A female kid is a girl. Some guys give up early in life, surrender completely before the impassable transparent wall, and remain little kids forever. . . .

The rest of us have to claw our way into Life as best we can, never knowing when we'll be Admitted. It happens to each of us in different ways—and once it does, there's no turning back.

It happened to me at the age of twelve in Northern Indiana—a remarkably barren terrain resembling in some ways the surface of the moon, encrusted with steel mills, oil refineries, and honky-tonk bars. There was plenty of natural motivation for Total Escape. Some kids got hung up on kite flying, others on pool playing. I became the greatest vicarious angler in the history of the Western world.

I say vicarious because there just wasn't any actual fishing to be done around where I lived. So I would stand for hours in front of the goldfish tank at Woolworth's, landing fantails in my mind, after incredible struggles. I read *Field & Stream, Outdoor Life,* and *Sports Afield* the way other kids read *G-8 And His Battle Aces*. I would break out in a cold sweat reading about these guys portaging to Alaska and landing rare salmon; and about guys climbing the High Sierras to do battle with the wily golden trout; and mortal combat with the steelheads. I'd read about craggy, sinewy sportsmen who discover untouched bass lakes where they have to beat off the pickerel with an oar, and the saber-toothed, raging smallmouths chase them ashore and right up into the woods.

After reading one of these fantasies I would walk around in a daze for hours, feeling the cork pistol grip of my imaginary trusty six-foot split-bamboo bait-casting rod in my right hand and hearing the high-pitched scream of my Pflueger Supreme reel straining to hold a seventeen-pound Great Northern in check.

I became known around town as "the-kid-who-is-the-nut-on-fishing," even went to the extent of learning how to tie flies, although I'd never been fly casting in my life. I read books on the subject. And in my bedroom, while the other kids are making balsa models of Curtiss Robins, I am busy tying Silver Doctors, Royal Coachmen, and Black Gnats. They were terrible. I would try out one in the bathtub to see whether it made a ripple that might frighten off the wily rainbow.

"Glonk!"

Down to the bottom like a rock, my floating dry fly would go. Fishing was part of the mysterious and unattainable Adult world. I wanted In.

My Old Man was In, though he was what you might call a once-in-a-while-fisherman-and-beer-party-goer; they are the same thing in the shadow of the blast furnaces. (I knew even then that there are people who Fish and there are people who Go Fishing; they're two entirely different creatures.) My Old Man did not drive fifteen hundred miles to the Atlantic shore with three thousand pounds of Abercrombie & Fitch fishing tackle to angle for stripers. He was the kind who would Go Fishing maybe once a month during the summer when it was too hot to Go Bowling and all of the guys down at the office would get The Itch. To them, fishing was a way of drinking a lot of beer and yelling. And getting away from the women. To me, it was a sacred thing. To *fish*.

He and these guys from the office would get together and go down to one of the lakes a few miles from where we lived—but never to Lake Michigan, which wasn't far away. I don't know why; I guess it was too big and awesome. In any case, nobody ever really thought of fishing in it. At least nobody in my father's mob. They went mostly to a mudhole known as Cedar Lake.

I will have to describe to you what a lake in the summer in Northern Indiana is like. To begin with, heat, in Indiana, is something else again. It descends like a three hundred-pound fat lady onto a picnic bench in the middle of July. It can literally be sliced into chunks and stored away in the basement to use in winter; on cold days you just bring it out and turn it on. Indiana heat is not a meteorological phenomenon—it is a solid element, something you can grab by the handles. Almost every day in the summer the whole town is just shimmering in front of you. You'd look across the street and skinny people would be all fat and wiggly like in the fun-house mirrors at Coney Island. The asphalt in the streets would bubble and hiss like a pot of steaming Ralston.

That kind of heat and sun produces mirages. All it takes is good flat country, a nutty sun, and insane heat and, by George, you're looking at Cleveland two hundred miles away. I remember many times standing out in center field on an incinerating day in mid-August, the prairie stretching out endlessly in all directions, and way out past the swamp would be this kind of tenuous, shadowy, cloud-like thing shimmering just above the horizon. It would be the Chicago skyline, upside down, just hanging there in the sky. And after a while it would gradually disappear.

So, naturally, fishing is different in Indiana. The muddy lakes, about May, when the sun starts beating down on them, would begin to simmer and bubble quietly around the edges. These lakes are not fed by springs or streams. I don't know what feeds them. Maybe seepage. Nothing but weeds and truck axles on the bottom; flat, low, muddy banks, surrounded by cottonwood trees, cattails, smelly marshes, and old dumps. Archetypal dumps. Dumps gravitate to Indiana lakes like flies to a hog killing. Way down at the end where the water is shallow and soupy are the old cars and the ashes, busted refrigerators, oil drums, old corsets, and God knows what else.

At the other end of the lake is the Roller Rink. There's *always* a Roller Rink. You can hear that old electric organ going, playing "Heartaches," and you can bear the sound of the roller skates:

"Shhhhhh . . . sssshhhhhhhhh . . . sssssshhhhhhhhhhhhhhh. . . ."

And the fistfights breaking out. The Roller Rink Nut in heat. The Roller Rink Nut was an earlier incarnation of the Drive-In Movie Nut. He was the kind who was very big with stainless steel diners, motels, horror movies, and frozen egg rolls. A close cousin to the Motorcycle Clod, he went ape for chicks with purple eyelids. You know the crowd. Crewcuts, low foreheads, rumbles, hollering, belching, drinking beer, roller skating on one foot, wearing black satin jackets with SOUTH SIDE A. C. lettered in white on the back around a white-winged roller-skated foot. The kind that hangs the stuff in the back windows of their '53 Mercuries; a huge pair of foam-rubber dice, a skull and crossbones, hula-hula dolls, and football players—Pro, of course, with heads that bob up and down. The guys with ball fringe around the windows of their cars, with phony Venetian blinds in the back, and big white rubber mudguards hanging down, with red reflectors. Or they'll take some old heap and line it with plastic imitation mink fur, pad the steering wheel with leopard skin and ostrich feathers until it weighs seventeen pounds and is as fat as a salami. A TV set, a bar, and a folding Castro bed are in the trunk, automatically operated and all lined with tasteful Sears Roebuck ermine. You know the crew—a true American product. We turn them out like Campbell's Pork & Beans.

This is the system of aesthetics that brought the Roller Rink to Cedar Lake, Indiana, when I was a kid.

About 150 yards from the Roller Rink was the Cedar Lake Evening In Paris Dance Hall. Festering and steamy and thronged with yeasty refugees from the Roller Rink. These are the guys who can't skate. But they can do other things. They're down there jostling back and forth in four hundred-percent humidity to the incomparable sounds of an Indiana dancehall band. Twelve non-Union cretinous musicians—Mickey Iseley's Moonlight Serenaders—blowing "Red Sails In the Sunset" on Montgomery Ward altos. The lighting is a tasteful combination of naked light bulbs, red and blue crepe paper, and orange cellophane gels.

In between the Roller Rink and the Dance Hall are seventeen small shacks known as Beer Halls. And surrounding this tiny oasis of civilization, this bastion of bonhomie, is a gigantic sea of total darkness, absolute pitch-black Stygian darkness, around this tiny island of totally decadent, bucolic American merriment. The roller skates are hissing, the beer bottles are crashing, the chicks are squealing, Mickey's reed men are quavering, and Life is full.

And in the middle of the lake, several yards away, are over seventeen thousand fishermen, in wooden rowboats rented at a buck and a half an hour. It is 2:00 A.M. The temperature is 175, with humidity to match. And the smell of decayed toads, the dumps at the far end of the lake, and an occasional *soupçon* of Standard Oil, whose refinery is a couple of miles away, is enough to put hair on the back of a mud turtle. Seventeen thousand guys clumped together in the middle, fishing for the known sixty-four crappies in that lake.

Crappies are a special breed of Midwestern fish, created by God for the express purpose of surviving in waters that would kill a bubonic-plague bacillus. They have never been known to fight, or even faintly struggle. I guess when you're a crappie, you figure it's no use anyway. One thing is as bad as another. They're just down there in the soup. No one quite knows what they eat, if anything, but everybody's fishing for them. At two o'clock in the morning.

Each boat contains a minimum of nine guys and fourteen cases of beer. And once in a while, in the darkness, is heard the sound of a guy falling over backward into the slime:

SSSSGLUNK!

"Oh! Ah! Help, help!" A piteous cry in the darkness. Another voice:

"Hey, for God's sake, Charlie's fallen in again! Grab the oar!"

And then it slowly dies down. Charlie is hauled out of the goo and is lying on the bottom of the boat, urping up dead lizards and Atlas Prager. Peace reigns again.

The water in these lakes is not the water you know about. It is composed of roughly ten percent waste glop spewed out by Shell, Sinclair, Phillips, and the Grasselli Chemical Corporation; twelve percent used detergent; thirty-five percent thick gruel composed of decayed garter snakes, deceased toads, fermenting crappies, and a strange, unidentifiable liquid that holds it all together. No one is quite sure *what* that is, because everybody is afraid to admit what it really is. They don't want to look at it too closely.

So this mélange lays there under the sun, and about August it is slowly simmering like a rich mulligatawny stew. At two in the morning you can hear the water next to the boat in the darkness:

"Gluuummp . . . Bluuuummmp."

Big bubbles of some unclassified gas come up from the bottom and burst. The natives, in their superstitious way, believe that it is highly inflammable. They take no chances.

The saddest thing of all is that on these lakes there are usually about nineteen summer cottages to the square foot, each equipped with a large motorboat. The sound of a 40-horsepower Chris-Craft going through a sea of number-ten oil has to be heard to be believed.

RRRRRRRAAAAAAAAHHHHHHHHHWWWWWWWWWWWRRRRRRRRRRR!

The prow is sort of parting the stuff, slowly stirring it into a sluggish, viscous wake.

Natives actually *swim* in this water. Of course, it is impossible to swim near the shore, because the shore is one great big sea of mud that goes all the way down to the core of the earth. There are stories of whole towns being swallowed up and stored in the middle of the earth. So the native rows out to the middle of the lake and hurls himself off the back seat of his rowboat.

"GLURP!"

It is impossible to sink in this water. The specific gravity and surface tension make the Great Salt Lake seem dangerous for swimming. You don't sink. You just bounce a little and float there. You literally have to hit your head on the surface of these lakes to get under a few inches. Once you do, you come up streaming mosquito eggs and dead toads—an Indiana specialty—and all sorts of fantastic things which are the offshoot of various exotic merriments which occur outside the Roller Rink.

The bottom of the lake is composed of a thick incrustation of old beer cans. The beer cans are at least a thousand feet thick in certain places.

And so seventeen thousand fishermen gather in one knot, because it is rumored that here is where The Deep Hole is. All Indiana lakes have a Deep Hole, into which, as the myth goes, the fish retire to sulk in the hot weather. Which is always.

Every month or so an announcement would be made by my Old Man, usually on a Friday night, after work.

"I'm getting up early tomorrow morning. I'm going fishing."

Getting up early and going fishing with Hairy Gertz and the crowd meant getting out of the house about three o'clock in the afternoon, roughly. Gertz was a key member of the party. He owned the Coleman lamp. It was part of the folklore that if you had a bright lantern in your boat the fish could not resist it. The idea was to hold the lantern out over the water and the fish would have to come over to see what was going on. Of course, when the fish arrived, there would be your irresistible worm, and that would be it.

Well, these Coleman lamps may not have drawn fish, but they worked great on mosquitoes. One of the more yeasty experiences in Life is to occupy a tiny rented rowboat with eight other guys, knee-deep in beer cans, with a blinding Coleman lamp hanging out of the boat, at 2:00 A.M., with the lamp hissing like Fu Manchu about to strike and every mosquito in the Western Hemisphere descending on you in the middle of Cedar Lake.

ZZZZZZZZZZZZZZZZZZTTTTTTTTTTTT

They *love* Coleman lamps. In the light they shed the mosquitoes swarm like rain. And in the darkness all around there'd be other lights in other boats, and once in a while a face would float above one. Everyone is coated with an inch and a half of something called citronella, reputedly a mosquito repellent but actually a sort of mosquito salad dressing.

The water is absolutely flat. There has not been a breath of air since April. It is now August. The surface is one flat sheet of old used oil laying in the darkness, with the sounds of the Roller Rink floating out over it, mingling with the angry drone of the mosquitoes and muffled swearing from the other boats. A fistfight breaks out at the Evening In Paris. The sound of sirens can be heard faintly in the Indiana blackness. It gets louder and then fades away. Tiny orange lights bob over the dance floor.

"Raaahhhhhd sails in the sawwwwnnnnsehhhht. . . . "

It's the drummer who sings. He figures some day Ted Weems will be driving by, and hear him, and. . . .

". . . haaaahhhhwwww brightlyyyy they shinneee. . . ."

There is nothing like a band vocalist in a rotten, struggling Mickey band. When you've heard him over two thousand yards of soupy, oily water, filtered through fourteen billion feeding mosquitoes in the August heat, he is particularly juicy and ripe. He is overloading the ten-watt Allied Radio Knight amplifier by at least four hundred percent, the gain turned all the way up, his chrome-plated bullet-shaped crystal mike on the edge of feedback.

"Raaahhhhhd sails in the sawwwwnnnnsehhhht. . . . "

It is the sound of the American night. And to a twelve-year-old kid it is exciting beyond belief.

Then my Old Man, out of the blue, says to me:

"You know, if you're gonna come along, you got to clean the fish."

Gonna come along! My God! I wanted to go fishing more than anything else in the world, and my Old Man wanted to drink beer more than anything else in the world, and so did Gertz and the gang, and more than even *that*, they wanted to get away from all the women. They wanted to get out on the lake and tell dirty stories and drink beer and get eaten by mosquitoes; just sit out there and sweat and be Men. They wanted to get away from work, the car payments, the lawn, the mill, and everything else.

And so here I am, in the dark, in a rowboat with The Men. I am half-blind with sleepiness. I am used to going to bed at nine-thirty or ten o'clock, and here it is two, three o'clock in the morning. I'm squatting in the back end of the boat, with eighty-seven million mosquitoes swarming over me, but I am *fishing!* I am out of my skull with fantastic excitement, hanging onto my pole.

In those days, in Indiana, they fished with gigantic cane poles. They knew not from Spinning. A cane pole is a long bamboo pole that's maybe twelve or fifteen feet in length; it weighs a ton, and tied to the end of it is about thirty feet of thick green line, roughly half the weight of the average clothesline, three big lead sinkers, a couple of crappie hooks, and a bobber.

One of Sport's most exciting moments is when seven Indiana fishermen in the same boat simultaneously and without consulting one another decide to pull their lines out of the water and recast. In total darkness. First the pole, rising like a huge whip:

"Whoooooooooooooooop!"

Then the lines, whirling overhead:

"Wheeeeeeeeeeeeooooooooooo!"

And then:

"OH! FOR CHRISSAKE! WHAT THE HELL?"

CLUNK! CLONK!

Sound of cane poles banging together, and lead weights landing in the boat. And such brilliant swearing as you have never heard. Yelling, hollering, with somebody always getting a hook stuck in the back of his ear. And, of course, all in complete darkness, the Coleman lamp at the other end of the rowboat barely penetrating the darkness in a circle of three or four feet.

"Hey, for God's sake, Gertz, will ya tell me when you're gonna pull your pole up!? Oh, Jesus Christ, look at this mess!"

There is nothing worse than trying to untangle seven cane poles, two hundred feet of soggy green line, just as they are starting to hit in the other boats. Sound carries over water:

"Shhhhh! I got a bite!"

The fishermen with the tangled lines become frenzied. Fingernails are torn, hooks dig deeper into thumbs, and kids huddle terrified out of range in the darkness.

You have been sitting for twenty hours, and nothing. A bobber just barely visible in the dark water is one of the most beautiful sights known to man. It's not doing anything, but there's always the feeling that at any instant it might. It just lays out there in the darkness. A luminous bobber, a beautiful thing, with a long, thin quill and a tiny red-and-white float, with just the suggestion of a line reaching into the black water. These are special bobbers for very tiny fish.

I have been watching my bobber so hard and so long in the darkness that I am almost hypnotized. I have not had a bite—ever—but the excitement of being there is enough for me, a kind of delirious joy that has nothing to do with sex or any of the more obvious pleasures. To this day, when I hear some guy singing in that special drummer's voice, it comes over me. It's two o'clock in the morning again. I'm a kid. I'm tired. I'm excited. I'm having the time of my life.

And at the other end of the lake:

"Raaahhhhd sails in the sawwwwnnnnnsehhhht. . . ."

The Roller Rink drones on, and the mosquitoes are humming. The Coleman lamp sputters, and we're all sitting together in our little boat.

Not really together, since I am a kid, and they are Men, but at least I'm there. Gertz is stewed to the ears. He is down at the other end. He has this fantastic collection of rotten stories, and early in the evening my Old Man keeps saying:

"There's a kid with us, you know."

But by two in the morning all of them have had enough so that it doesn't matter. They're telling stories, and I don't care. I'm just sitting there, clinging to my cane pole when, by God, I get a nibble!

I don't believe it. The bobber straightens up, jiggles, dips, and comes to rest in the gloom. I whisper:

"I got a bite!"

The storytellers look up from their beer cans in the darkness.

"What . . . ? Hey, whazzat?"

"Shhhhh! Be quiet!"

We sit in silence, everybody watching his bobber through the haze of insects. The drummer is singing in the distance. We hang suspended for long minutes. Then suddenly all the bobbers dipped and went under. The crappies are hitting!

You never saw anything like it! We are pulling up fish as fast as we can get them off the hooks. Crappies are flying into the boat, one after the other, and hopping around on the bottom in the darkness, amid the empty beer cans. Within twenty minutes we have landed forty-seven fish. We are knee-deep in crappies. The jackpot!

Well, the Old Man just goes wild. They are all yelling and screaming and pulling the fish in—while the other boats around us are being skunked. The fish have come out of their hole or whatever it is that they are in at the bottom of the lake, the beer cans and the old tires, and have decided to eat.

You can hear the rest of the boats pulling up anchors and rowing over, frantically. They are thumping against us. There's a big, solid phalanx of wooden boats around us. You could walk from one boat to the other for miles around. And still they are skunked. We are catching the fish!

By 3:00 A.M. they've finally stopped biting, and an hour later we are back on land. I'm falling asleep in the rear seat between Gertz and Zudock. We're driving home in the dawn, and the men are hollering, drinking, throwing beer cans out on the road, and having a great time.

We are back at the house, and my father says to me as we are coming out of the garage with Gertz and the rest of them:

"And now Ralph's gonna clean the fish. Let's go in the house and have something to eat. Clean 'em on the back porch, will ya, kid?"

In the house they go. The lights go on in the kitchen; they sit down and start eating sandwiches and making coffee. And I am out on the back porch with forty-seven live, flopping crappies.

They are well named. Fish that are taken out of muddy, rotten, lousy, stinking lakes are muddy, rotten, lousy, stinking fish. It is as simple as that. And they are made out of some kind of hard rubber.

I get my Scout knife and go to work. Fifteen minutes and twenty-one crappies later I am sick over the side of the porch. But I do not stop. It is part of Fishing.

By now, nine neighborhood cats and a raccoon have joined me on the porch, and we are all working together. The August heat, now that we are away from the lake, is even hotter. The uproar in the kitchen is getting louder and louder. There is nothing like a motley collection of Indiana office workers who have just successfully defeated Nature and have brought home the kill. Like cave men of old, they celebrate around the campfire with song and drink. And belching.

I have now finished the last crappie and am wrapping the clean fish in the editorial page of the *Chicago Tribune*. It has a very tough paper that doesn't leak. Especially the editorial page.

The Old Man hollers out:

"How you doing? Come in and have a Nehi."

I enter the kitchen, blinded by that big yellow light bulb, weighted down with a load of five-and-a-half-inch crappies, covered with fish scales and blood, and smelling like the far end of Cedar Lake. There are worms under my fingernails from baiting hooks all night, and I am feeling at least nine feet tall. I spread the fish out on the sink—and old Hairy Gertz says:

"My God! Look at those *speckled beauties!*" An expression he had picked up from *Outdoor Life*.

The Old Man hands me a two-pound liverwurst sandwich and a bottle of Nehi orange. Gertz is now rolling strongly, as are the other eight file clerks, all smelly, and mosquito-bitten, eyes red-rimmed from the Coleman lamp, covered with worms and with the drippings of at least fifteen beers apiece. Gertz hollers:

"Ya know, lookin' at them fish reminds me of a story." He is about to uncork his cruddiest joke of the night. They all lean forward over the white enamel kitchen table with the chipped edges, over the salami and the beer bottles, the rye bread and the mustard. Gertz digs deep into his vast file of obscenity.

"One time there was this Hungarian bartender, and ya know, he had a cross-eyed daughter and a bowlegged dachshund. And this. . . ."

At first I am holding back, since I am a kid. The Old Man says:

"Hold it down, Gertz. You'll wake up the wife and she'll raise hell."

He is referring to My Mother.

Gertz lowers his voice and they all scrunch their chairs forward amid a great cloud of cigar smoke. There is only one thing to do. I scrunch forward, too, and stick my head into the huddle, right next to the Old Man, into the circle of leering, snickering, fishy-smelling faces. Of course, I do not even remotely comprehend the gist of the story. But I know that it is rotten to the core.

Gertz belts out the punch line; the crowd bellows and beats on the table. They begin uncapping more Blatz.

Secretly, suddenly, and for the first time, I realize that I am In. The Eskimo pies and Nehi oranges are all behind me, and a whole new world is stretching out endlessly and wildly in all directions before me. I have gotten The Signal!

Suddenly my mother is in the doorway in her Chinese-red chenille bathrobe. Ten minutes later I am in the sack, and out in the kitchen Gertz is telling another one. The bottles are rattling, and the file clerks are hunched around the fire celebrating their primal victory over The Elements.

Somewhere off in the dark the Monon Louisville Limited wails as it snakes through the Gibson Hump on its way to the outside world. The giant Indiana moths, at least five pounds apiece, are banging against the window screens next to my bed. The cats are fighting in the backyard over crappie heads, and fish scales are itching in my hair as I joyfully, ecstatically slide off into the great world beyond.

an excerpt from

Nothing but Blue Skies

Thomas McGuane

Serious fly fishermen are exceptionally lucky when one of our great novelists writes about the sport. With their impeccable hand at language and narrative, they often avoid the technicalities of a sport that can drown you in them. With restraint and loving care, and a constant eye to the larger purposes of this scene between father and daughter on a Montana river, Thomas McGuane etches a memorable portrait unique to the sport.
—NL

The sun was just coming up. They could make out the light in the tops of cottonwoods. And dropping smoothly out of sight was the pale disc of the moon with its wonderful discolorations. It was like being in a big church in the middle of the week and the only light was in the high windows. They put their rods together and leaned them against the hood of the Buick. Frank opened the bag of doughnuts and set them out and Holly poured coffee from the steel thermos.

"It's already warm," she said. She screwed the lid back on the thermos and set it down decisively. The steam curled up from their cups. There was a dusting of powdered sugar from the doughnuts on the black paint of the hood.

"It was good we started early."

Holly turned her head and listened. Then Frank heard it, a coyote insinuating a thin pure note that seemed to fade into the sky. He could almost feel himself carried with it into a pure blue place. "Are you going to take a net?" Holly asked. She still cocked her head in the direction of the coyote. She smiled to indicate that she had heard it. The little wolves had been here for thousands of years.

"I don't think so. The lanyard always stretches in the brush and fires the damn thing into my kidneys. You know what, though? Maybe I better. Think if we hooked a big one somewhere we couldn't beach it."

"Gosh this coffee is good. Didn't that 'yote sound pretty?"

"Beautiful."

"Beautiful. . . . That's right, beautiful."

Frank went ahead and found a cow trail through the wild roses with their modest pink blossoms. The cottonwoods left off quickly and they were on a broad level place. Here and there were stands of cattails, water just out of sight. And while they threaded their way on a game trail through the brush, they could hear waterfowl chatting among themselves about their passage. When they were almost to the stream, they walked under a huge dead cottonwood, a splendid outreaching candelabra shape festooned with ravens who nervously strode their perches and croaked at the humans beneath them. One bird pirouetted from his branch and, falling like a black leaf, settled on the trail ahead of them. They stopped and Frank tossed his last piece of doughnut. The raven hopped up to it, picked it up in his beak, flew back with it to his roost. "This isn't his first day on the job," said Frank.

Before they reached the edge of the stream the sun was upon them. There was no bank as such, just the end of the wild roses and an uplifted ridge of thorn trees where magpies squawked at the intrusion. But they could hear the stream, which emanated not far away from a series of blue spring holes at a water temperature that stayed constant, winter and summer. Frank loved to arrive at a stream he knew as well as this one. You could strike it at any point and know where you were, like opening a favorite book at a random page.

They stopped at the edge and gazed upon the deep silky current. A pair of kingbirds fought noisily across the stream, and on its banks were intermittent pale purple stands of wild iris. Holly said, "Ah." For some reason she looked as small as a child in her chest waders; whenever she stopped, she stood her fly rod next to her as a soldier would, while Frank flicked at the irises with the tip of his. He stared at the steady flow of water.

"Nothing moving," Frank said. "Needs to warm up."

"Where is the otter pool from here?"

"Well, right above us is the long riffle—"

"With the foam buildup in the corner?"

"Yup, and then the long ledge with the plunge in the middle of it."

"Okay, I know where I am now. Otter pool right above that."

"Holly! We're a little foggy on details."

"I'm a history major. The foreground erodes for history majors. We like an alpine perspective."

They worked their way along the bank, blind casting to the undercut far side, hopscotching upstream until they could hear the shallow music of the riffle. Frank tried to watch Holly without making her self-conscious. She was an accurate close-range caster, her line a clean tight loop, and she had the ability to slow the line down, almost to the point of its falling when she was presenting the fly. She soon hooked a fish.

"What have you got on?" Frank asked as she fought the fish, her rod in a bow. The fish jumped high above the pool as they talked.

"Elk hair caddis. Just something that floats." She hunkered next to the bank and slipped her hand under the fish, a nice trout of about a pound. She let it go, stood up and smiled at Frank while she cast the line back and forth to dry her fly.

At the broad ledge they were each able to take a side of the stream and fish at the same time, casting up into the bubbled seam beneath the rocks. Holly pointed to the plunge at the center and said to Frank, "After you, my boy." Frank cast straight into the center of the plunge. The fly barely had time to land before he hooked a rainbow that blew end over end out into the shallows and held for a long time against the curve of his rod, a band of silver-pink ignited by the morning light. Soon Frank had it in hand, a hard cold shape, gazing down at the water while he freed the hook. Frank let it go and rinsed his hand. He looked upstream and said, "The otter pool."

"You forgot to thank me for that fish."

"Thank you, Holly."

The sun was still too low, and so they waited quietly before they started upstream. The tall sedges grew down so close to the bank that it was necessary for them to stay in the stream to get up to the otter pool. They waded in the center where the current had scrubbed the bottom down to firm sand. Frank was in over his hips and Holly was almost to the top of her waders. She held her rod up in the air and pressed the top of her waders to her chest with her free hand so that water couldn't splash in. They made two great Vs in the current. "This is the moon," said Holly, "and I'm on tiptoes."

"Smell the cold air on the surface of the river."

"Stop," said Holly, peering closely at the water. They were on either side of the thread of current and mayflies were starting to appear, unfurling their tiny wings and struggling to float upright. Every few seconds one would come by, some still in their nymphal stage, the case just beginning to split and release the furled wing; others were sailing upright like pale yellow sloops.

"*Ephemerella infrequens*," said Holly.

"Little sulphurs," said Frank.

"Pale morning duns," said Holly, "like I told you last night."

Frank hung on to his old names for flies, had never learned the Latin of Holly's generation of anglers. "Pale morning dun" was the compromise, reasonably objective compared to the sulphurs and yellow sallies and hellgrammites and blue-winged olives of Frank's upbringing.

At the bend, the wild irises looked as if they would topple into the stream. The narrow band of mud at the base of the sedges revealed a well-used muskrat trail, and on this band stood a perfectly motionless blue heron, head back like the hammer of a gun. It flexed its legs slightly, croaked, sprang into wonderfully slow flight, a faint whistle of pinions, then disappeared over the top of the wall of grasses as though drawn down into its mass.

Around this bend was the otter pool, so called because, when Holly was twelve, she and Frank had watched a family of river otters, three of them, pursuing trout in its depths. Holly took the position that the otters were just like their family: one otter was Frank, one Holly, one Gracie. When the three seized the same trout and rent it, Holly cried, "Oh, poor trout!" and sent the otters into panicked flight upstream.

They stopped quietly at the lower end of the pool, which was wide and deep and surrounded by aspens and cottonwoods. At the top of the pool was a rocky run that looked like a watery stairway. It enlivened a silvery chute of bubbles that didn't disperse until a third of the way down the pool. The movement of water folded into a precise seam of current only at the end of the pool. All along the seam, trout were rising and sipping down the mayflies under a tapestry of reflected cottonwood leaves.

They stopped to watch. "Hm," said Holly.

"An embarrassment of riches."

As they watched, a fish rose about halfway up the pool, a quiet rise that displaced more water than the others, sending a tremor out toward the sides of the pool. Holly grabbed his arm.

"See that?" she asked.

"Mm-hm."

The fish rose again and, in a minute, again.

"Has it got a feeding rhythm," Holly asked, "or is it just taking them when they come?" The fish rose again, its dorsal making a slight thread against the surface.

"I think it's on a rhythm. There're just too many bugs coming off now. What kind of leader have you got on?"

"Twelve-footer, 5X," Holly said. "You're not going to make me cast to that thing, are you?"

"Didn't I thank you for that last rainbow?"

"Can I get by with this tippet?"

"You'll have to. I hate to take the time to change it now. I don't know if you could hold this fish with anything lighter, assuming you make the cast."

"Assuming I make the cast . . . "

A light breeze moved across the water and turned it from black to silver, a faint corrugation that obscured everything that was happening. "Right-hand wind," Holly said gloomily. Then it went back to slick black. "Am I going to line those little fish, trying to reach him?"

"I think you've got to take that chance," said Frank, easing over to the bank in a slight retreat to the ledge where the heron had stood. "If you think about them too much, it'll throw you off." The fish fed again. Even Frank had a nervous stomach. Holly stood and stared. Frank said, "I'm going to try to get up the bank where I can see this fish better. Why don't you try to get in position?"

Frank left his rod at the side of the stream and pushed his way through grass as tall as his face until he got up onto the top of the bank. He worked his way back through the brush until he could look back and see the pool glinting through the branches. Then he got on all fours and crawled to the slight elevation alongside the pool. By the time he reached it, he was on his belly and perfectly concealed. He could see right into the middle of the pool. "Ready to call in the artillery," he said.

"I can't even see you," said Holly.

"Nothing going on."

"Do you think he's gone?"

"No."

Small fish continued making their splashy rises. Frank could see well enough to make out the insects. He rested his chin on the backs of his hands and didn't have to wait long. He tracked a dun mayfly out of the bubbles at the head of the pool, then another, then another. When this one reached mid-pool, a shape arose, clarified into a male brown trout with a distinct hook to its lower jaw and sipped the fly off the surface. It was a startlingly big fish, leopard-spotted, with its prominent dorsal fin piercing the surface. The low pale curve of its belly appeared to grow out of the depths of the pool itself. It sank almost from sight, but even after it had fed, Frank could make out its observing presence deep in the pool, a kind of intelligence.

"See that?"

Instead of answering, Holly began to strip line from her reel. She had the fly in her hand and blew on it. "I'm just going to cast," she said. "I'm thinking too hard. How big?"

"Big."

"Oh, I wish I hadn't asked."

"You have the fish marked pretty well?"

"Yeah, here goes."

Frank could see her false casting, but the fly tailed the loop, turned over too soon and hooked on the line. "Shit!" Holly brought her line back in and cleared the fly.

"You're rushing, Holly. You're turning it over too soon. Cast like you always do. Don't press." She started again. "Slow, slow." And she did, resuming her elegant cadence. The curve of line opened. The fly floated down and the fish arose steadily from the depths. "Whoa whoa whoa," said Frank. "Don't strike, he's taking one in front of yours. Let the current take your fly away." The fish eased up, made a seam as he broke the surface, then sank. Frank heard a pent-up breath escape from Holly while he watched the heavy fish suck an insect down. The fish held just beneath the surface, both the dorsal and tip of his tail out of the water; his gills flared crimson and a faint turbulence spread to the surface from either side of his head.

"Try again while he's still up," Frank said, and an instant later Holly's fly fluttered down from above, right in the feeding lane of the trout. He could see the fly rock around on the bright hackles Holly had wound on the hook last night, slowly closing on the fish. The trout elevated slowly and the fly disappeared down a tiny whirlpool in the water. "There," said Frank, not too loud, and the thin leader tightened into the air, a pale cool spray the length of it. "You've got him!"

Frank stood straight up out of the brush as the trout surged across the pool.

Holly held her rod high with both hands and said, "Oh, God God God God God."

"Let him go."

"I *am* letting him go."

"Don't touch that reel."

"I'm not touching the reel!"

Frank got back below the pool and waded out to Holly. The reel was screeching. She was looking straight ahead where the line pointed. There was a deep bow in the rod. She moved her face slightly in Frank's direction. "I'm dying," she said. The fish started to run and the click of the reel set up a steady howl. "I am going to die."

Frank wanted to take some of the pressure off Holly. He moved his ear next to the screeching reel and looked up at her. "Darling," he said, "they're playing our song."

"Daddy, stop it. This is killing me!"

"I thought this was supposed to be fun."

"It's torture. Oh, God."

The fish stayed in the pool. It might have sensed that Frank and Holly were at the lower end, and the rapids above were probably too shallow for a fish this big to negotiate. If it went that way, the light leader would have quickly broken on rocks. All Holly could do was keep steady pressure and hope the fish was well hooked and that none of its teeth were close to the tippet. She was doing her part perfectly. The fish began to work its way deliberately around the pool, staying deep. "I guess this is where we get to see if there are any snags," she said gloomily. This fish swam entirely around the pool once, an extraordinarily smart thing to do; but it couldn't find something to wind Holly's leader around. And it was having increasing difficulty staying deep in the pool. Holly continued to keep the same arc in her rod and watched vigilantly where the line sliced the surface. Finally, the fish stopped and held, then slowly let itself be lifted toward the surface. For the first time, Holly cautiously reeled.

Frank undid his net from the back of his vest and held it in the water to wet the mesh. The fish was coming toward them. "Let me be in front of you, Hol," he said quietly. When the fish was closer, he held the net underwater toward the fish. He could hear the unhurried turns of the reel handle. He looked straight at the fish from above. It turned quietly around and went back to the center of the pool, accompanied by the steady whine of Holly's reel. "Oh, how much of this can I stand!" said Holly. But when the fish stopped, she resumed her steady work.

"We'll catch this fish, Hol."

"Do you think so?"

"I think so."

"You're just saying that, aren't you?"

"No, I foresee the fish in my net."

When the fish reappeared, Frank stared hard and moved the net toward it. The fish seemed pressed away by the net. Holly brought it closer and the net pushed it away but it didn't move off quite the same way. "I'm going for it," Holly said, and pulled hard enough to move the fish toward Frank; the fish turned and chugged toward the other bank but was unable to dive. Holly brought it back once more, and this time the fish glided toward the pressure of her rod and Frank swept the net in the air, streaming silver and slung deeply with the bright spotted weight of the fish.

"I'm so happy, I'm so happy!" Holly cried as Frank submerged the net to keep the trout underwater. "I never caught such a big fish!" "He slipped his hand inside the net and around the slick underside of the trout, unveiling him delicately as the net was lifted clear. With his left hand under the fish and his right hand around its tall, he was able to hold it. The little pale yellow fly was stuck just in the edge of his upper jaw. Holly reached down to free it and the fly fell out at her touch. Frank held the fish head up into the current until the kicks of the tail became strong. "You want to do the honors?" he asked.

"You."

"Grab," he said. Holly took the wrist of the fish's tail just above Frank's hand.

Holly let go, then Frank let go, feeling the weight of the fish with his left hand and the curve of the fish's belly with his right. Underwater, the trout seemed to take its bearings and balance itself. Then it kicked free, gliding to disappear into the middle of the pool. They began hollering like wild hog hunters, gesturing at the sky, Frank with his fists, Holly with her rod.

"I'm the champion of the world!" Holly yelled.

There seemed little point in doing anything but contemplate the bewildering size of a trout that must have rarely let down its guard in a long life. They were confident it would never make that mistake again. It was strange to feel affection for a creature finning secretively, almost below the light, disturbing the gravel bottom with an outrush of water from its broad gills. They were silent in the glitter of cottonwood leaves.

Later, as they drove home, they sang. Frank pushed off the steering wheel to belt out his small part and Holly twisted in her seat operatically.

"Hey!"

"Hey!"

"You!"

"You!"

"Get offa my cloud!"

And Holly's visit home was over. When her plane went off in a shrinking silver spot that disappeared, he felt his chest go all fluid with emotion that rose up through his face before he controlled it. With so many of his family, people he had known, gone, to have someone he loved as much as he loved Holly poised early in her life, facing out onto the flat earth, was overwhelming. Today he had had her attention fully and he knew that wouldn't always be true. It was hard to take that in.

Fly Fishing Folly

Ailm Travler

*"Fly fishing is a way of hooking into the world," says Ailm Travler in this
stunning essay on deeper meanings in an old sport: it is "useless, unreasonable, irrational,
and without purpose"; it "turns survival into an art"; it imps the laws of poetry;
it is folly—and it is, in its catching and then releasing fish,
"letting the cycle continue." She's terrific.*
—NL

Fly fishing twists fate like a dream and together with wildness, makes anything possible. Wildness dances at the edge of nonsense and catastrophe: a thunderstorm comes out of nowhere on a high alpine lake, and snow follows heat lightning; a forest fire sweeps a hillside and new shoots sprout green in spring; a searing drought sucks creeks and rivers dry that just last year were home to hundreds of spawning trout. Fly fishing both nurtures wildness and transforms it.

When I go fishing I deliberately go to a place I don't know yet. It would be easy to fish the same waters week after week, to drive to a place where I could catch "stockers," those predictable rainbows dumped out of steel drums for creel addicts. But that's not the idea. I want to make it hard for myself, mysterious, a shape-shifting journey to another world where I can turn into a wild trout.

Journeys to the world of wild trout take me to places where survival hangs in the balance. Wild trout depend upon a yearly and seasonal life cycle of thousands of insects, and they can survive only in clear, cold streams recharged by snows and rains, streams that are not overly acidic. And wild trout are endangered by those who dam rivers for profit, turn mountainsides into board-feet and use radar screens to catch fish.

The loss of pristine trout waters makes fishing hard. Fly fishing makes fishing even harder by demanding an attention to minutiae that is archaic. It requires an intimacy with bugs, birds, weather, water, and fish that sticking a worm on a hook never asked of me.

I have to squint at a tiny fly of feather and fur pinched between my cold fingers; I get a headache trying to tie the fly onto a piece of hair-thin gut. Then I am forced to slide on my stomach through thorny gooseberry bushes, step into the ooze of a bog or over sharp rocks and boulders so that the trout won't see me. For what?

To touch something primordial and strange. To catch a glimpse of trout feeding in a pool beneath a waterfall, watch them dart out from a shadow to sip an emerging nymph or struggling caddis fly. To become water and stone, current and foam; to find myself alone at "the beginning," the time of creation, when animals, fish, birds, and fir trees spoke the same language.

Fly fishing is a way of hooking into the world, being part of the swirling current and riffle patterns on a river, the tall grasses bending down into pocket water; the chill, the sun, the quiet or the screech of hawks. You become what you fish: a vulnerable cutthroat in a brushy, steep mountain stream; a sly brown hiding deep in the roiling waist-high waters of the Rio Grande; a skittish brookie in a meandering meadow creek; a wary golden trout in a deep alpine lake.

I do not have to fish in order to survive. Eating off the land is really possible only for those who have access to thousands of acres of wilderness year round. Surviving off the land is a rarity these days, and only a handful of indigenous peoples know how to do it.

The truth is, fly fishing is folly: useless, unreasonable, irrational, and without purpose. Fly fishing is folly precisely because it makes survival harder than it already is, and by doing so, turns survival into art.

Like poetry, fly fishing is evocative beyond thought—the rings of water after a rise.

Poetry may not be "useful," but its form obeys primordial laws of meter and rhythm. To utter the ineffable, one must retrace a journey to the beginning when meter and rhythm were born, the source of "a little language such as lovers use, words of one syllable." [1]

The same is true of fly fishing. Just as poetry obeys primordial laws, there is a canon of law in fly fishing: how to cast, what a fly should look like, how to read the water and so on. You have to learn to snap or flip the line in the air so that your fly lies perfectly on the water; you must know your knots, your entomology and the proper tippet for the proper leader.

But these are just the mechanics. The real requirement is to learn to think like a trout who, in a split second, sorts out a bunch of shape-shifting elements in order to survive. In that moment, gazing at the air above the water for whirring insects, parting stickling willow branches, peering at a glistening riffle for a shadow or in the tailspin smooth water behind a rock for a disappearing fin, the rules vanish and there is only a dream. Flip Splash. The hesitation after the trout strikes. You raise your arm to set the hook.

When the trout leaps out of the water to take the fly, there is silence. You

[1] From *The Waves,* Virginia Woolf.

don't know how you got there, standing half in the water, brush scratching at your cheek. A dream. The trout hits the water. The hush breaks, the leaves rustle again, the water flows again. A bird calls. The trout is tugging at your line, and you are transformed.

Like the heroes of great mythological quests, fishermen like to boast of the "big one" that got away and, more often, the big one that they caught. The fish's proportions are heroic, and as the fish is pursued, its size increases. In "fish stories," not only are the fish huge but the waters are teeming with them as well.

Back in 1947 me and Bill hiked up an old trail and fished this creek. We must have caught 110 fish!

July 12, 1890. Ralph and Grandfather went up to Shingle Bridge and brought back 240 trout.

The trouble is, those waters no longer exist. They've been sucked dry for irrigation, dammed up for electricity and silted into nonexistence by mining and logging. And if streams and lakes manage to escape this pummeling, they are overfished.

I was guilty of it. In the beginning I wanted to catch as many fish as possible. I even had a worm farm so that I would have an unlimited, free supply of worms in order to catch an unlimited amount of fish. A weighty knapsack full of trout wrapped in mint grass in a plastic bag and sputtering, crisp trout in the frying pan were the objectives of "going fishing." I'd break the rules and smile when I opened the freezer and saw all of those neatly wrapped packages of trout.

Then something happened. One spring I decided to get a fly rod. I don't know why. It was a feeling, a vague image of something that teased at me, drew me in, like the hexagram Youthful Folly in the I Ching, "It is not I who seek the young fool, the young fool seeks me."[2]

My desire to catch as many trout as possible didn't change in one season. It was when I started tying my own flies the following winter that I began to notice a transformation.

When I am sitting at the tying vise the world is focused on the space in front

---

[2] From Hexagram four, Meng/Youthful Folly, *The I Ching or Book of Changes.*

of me where dubbing furs, feathers, thread, and ribbing materials are spread out: deer, hare, and muskrat fur; rooster and hen hackles; peacock swords, pheasant tails; gold and silver tinsel; red and yellow floss; brown, black and cream thread. Everything else vanishes.

The hook in the vise represents the water the insect I am imitating hatches from, swims around in, flies out of, or falls into. The type of fly I tie chooses the weather, the shore, the stream, river, lake, or pond, the wind, sun, clouds, and, ultimately, the trout I want to catch. Once the fly is tied onto the tippet of my leader, it is more than an imitation insect, it is my guide to another world.

The idea behind fishing with a fly is to trick the trout into thinking your fly is a real insect. You get so tricky that pretty soon you forget why you are spending so many hours bent over a hook no bigger than a lettuce seed, and hours more retrieving the nicely camouflaged hook from brush, branches, and beaver dams. Expending that much effort at creating something elegant only to lose it on the underside of a boulder buried in the river or the top branches of a nearby juniper might be considered pain in the service of beauty. To do it week after week, season after season, is folly.

The spring which followed my fly-tying winter, I came full circle and found myself at the beginning of my journey, but now with folly as my guide, I knew "the place for the first time."[3]

Besides tying flies, I had also studied maps of northern New Mexico and southern Colorado, looking for places where nobody went, where I might find pristine waters teeming with fish all to myself. I located a protected wildlife area crisscrossed by two streams, inaccessible to all but mountain bikers and hikers with a lot of time.

One weekend, in the midst of a vicious drought, a friend and I put our bikes in the back of the pickup and drove a couple of hours until we came to an unassuming barbed wire fence and gate in the foothills of the Rockies. Before us lay a landscape of brown, stunted grasses, shriveled bushes and leafless trees. Blue-green mountains loomed in the distance.

[3] From "Little Gidding," *The Four Quartets*, T. S. Eliot.

It was suffocating, hot. We biked a few miles on a dirt road and then cut north, overland, bumping our way along overgrazed meadows and cow paths, in the direction of the first stream shown on the topographical map. We crossed a pitiful, dribbling sluice of warm water and headed for the forest, where the map showed a lake with a stream running into it.

When we got to where the lake was supposed to be it wasn't there. We pulled our bikes over fallen trees and up some ravines. We rode further, climbing steadily, in and out of aspen glades along the edge of pine and fir trees where we surprised elk napping in the shadows. Soon we were biking along a small creek flowing in the darkness of dense underbrush and willow thickets.

When the trace of a trail began a steep climb, we gave up and stopped. I had long ago lost the thrill of the bike adventure and wanted to fish. I put together my fly rod and tied on a small-sized parachute Adams I had tied that winter. I walked downstream a ways and then, crouching and crawling, fought my way through a tangle of willows and gooseberry bushes. When I finally reached the mossy banks of the creek and saw the crystal pools stepping their way upstream, I was entranced.

I moved closer, trying to stay invisible in the brush, and bent toward the first pool. The water was so low that the native cutthroat trout were bunched in the pockets of deep water formed behind fallen logs and cairns of mossy rocks. I tossed the fly onto the surface of the pool and with a splash and tug I had my first fish. It had been so easy that, after flipping out the hook, I gently let the cutthroat with its red-orange gills slide back into the water. It swam away in fright, but there was nowhere to go because the water was so low. Seconds later the trout was back in position behind the log, darting for food floating down the current.

I went to the next pool. The same thing. I lobbed my Adams gently onto the surface and strike! I released another speckled cutthroat. Trout after trout. I let them all go. I was excited. Success was coming so swiftly and easily. I reached a point near where my friend was reading under a tree. I waved her over, and we both crept into the brush upstream to a pool. I cast my fly into the current and a trout leapt out of the water to take it. My friend watched me let the fish go with amazement. I caught another. She congratulated me and went back to her book.

I scrambled upstream through the brush and peered down at the tailwater above a small waterfall. A bunch of cutthroat were holding in the deep water, waiting for a morsal. I put my rod aside. I took off my boots and rolled up my pants. Cautiously I stepped in the cool water. I splashed some on my face and sat down. The trout swam next to me unperturbed, treating me like a rock, a place to rest and wait for unsuspecting insects. We sat there. They finned, I was still. I watched them fish for nymphs and bugs. I was content.

I learned something that day, something about myself and the natural world and the fragility of ecosystems of which we humans are but a small part. It is not we who are the heroes with our fish stories, it is the trout themselves. They have managed to survive drought, selfishness, and greed.

I yearn for rivers and streams teeming with fish because I would love to be able to catch fish and bonk them on their heads without a care in the world. But even if those places did exist, and a few still do, I would let the trout go anyway. Catching and releasing wild trout is not just a sport or game, it is *letting the cycle continue*. Not trying to stop the wind or rain but letting it pass through. Success for me lies in wildness and wonder—the folly of releasing wild trout back into their cold, clear waters to grow old.

A Fly-Fishing Primer

P. J. O'Rourke

*Only P. J. O'Rourke, the quick-witted, acerbic political humorist, could write a line like
"here's a guy standing in cold water up to his liver throwing the world's most expensive
clothesline at trees." In just a few pages he pokes his rapier into the language,
the proper names, the mores of the sport, the cliches, and his own blundering.
And then something happens.*
—NL

I'd never fly-fished. I'd done other kinds of fishing. I'd fished for bass. That's where I'd get far enough away from the dock so that people couldn't see there wasn't any line on my pole, then drink myself blind in the rowboat. And I'd deep-sea fished. That's where the captain would get me blind before we'd even left the dock, and I'd be the one who couldn't see the line. But I'd never fly-fished.

I'd always been of two minds about the sport. On one hand, here's a guy standing in cold water up to his liver throwing the world's most expensive clothesline at trees. A full two-thirds of his time is spent untangling stuff, which he could be doing in the comfort of his own home with old shoelaces, if he wanted. The whole business costs like sin and requires heavier clothing. Furthermore, it's conducted in the middle of blackfly season. Cast and swat. Cast and swat. Fly fishing may be a sport invented by insects with fly fishermen as bait. And what does the truly sophisticated dry-fly artist do when he finally bags a fish? He lets the fool thing go and eats baloney sandwiches instead.

On the other hand, fly fishing did have its attractions. I love to waste time and money. I had ways to do this most of the year—hunting, skiing, renting summer houses in To-Hell-And-Gone Harbor for a Lebanon hostage's ransom. But, come spring, I was limited to cleaning up the yard. Even with a new Toro every two years and a lot of naps by the compost heap, it's hard to waste much time and money doing this. And then there's the gear needed for fly fishing. I'm a sucker for anything that requires more equipment than I have sense. My workshop is furnished with the full panoply of Black & Decker power tools, all bought for the building of one closet shelf in 1979.

When I began to think about fly fishing, I realized I'd never be content again until my den was cluttered with computerized robot fly-tying vises, space-age Teflon and ceramic knotless tapered leaders, sterling-silver English fish scissors, and thirty-five volumes on the home life of the midge. And there was one other thing. I'm a normal male who takes an occasional nip; therefore, I love to put funny things on my head. Sometimes it's the nut dish, sometimes the spaghetti colander, but the hats I'd seen fly fishermen wear were funnier than either, and I had to have one.

I went to Hackles & Tackle, an upscale dry-fly specialty shop that also sells fish-print wallpaper and cashmere V-neck sweaters with little trout on them. I got a graphite rod for about the price of a used car and a reel made out of the kind of exotic alloys that you can go to jail for selling to the Soviet Union. I also got one of those fishing vests that only comes down to the top of your beer gut and looks like you dressed in the dark and tried to put on your ten-year-old son's threepiece suit. And I purchased lots of monofilament and teensy hooks covered in auk down and moose lint and an entire L. L. Bean boat bag full of fly-fishing do-whats, hinky-doovers, and whachamajigs.

I also brought home a set of fly-fishing how-to video tapes. This is the eighties, I reasoned, the age of video. What better way to take up a sport than from a comfortable armchair? That's where I'm at my best with most sports anyway.

There were three tapes. The first one claimed it would teach me to cast. The second would teach me to "advanced cast." And the third would tell me where trout live, how they spend their weekends, and what they'd order for lunch if there were underwater delicatessens for fish. I started the VCR, and a squeaky little guy with an earnest manner and a double-funny hat came on, began heaving fly line around, telling me the secret to making beautiful casting loops is . . .

Whoever made these tapes apparently assumed I knew how to tie backing to reel and line to backing and leader to line and so on all the way out to the little feather and fuzz that fish sometimes eat at the end. I didn't even know how to put my rod together. I had to go to the children's section at the public library and check out *My Big Book of Fishing* and begin with how to open the package it all came in.

A triple granny got things started on the spool. After twelve hours and help from pop rivets and a tube of Crazy Glue, I managed an Albright knot between backing and line. But my version of a nail knot in the leader put Mr. Gordian of ancient-Greek-knot-legend fame strictly on the shelf. It was the size of a hamster and resembled one of the Wooly Bugger flies I'd bought, except it was in the size you use for killer whales. I don't want to talk about blood knots and tippets. There I was with two pieces of invisible plastic, trying to use fingers the size of jumbo hot dogs while holding a magnifying glass and a Tensor lamp between my teeth and gripping nasty tangles of monofilament with each big toe. My girl-friend had to come over and cut me out of this with pinking shears. I've decided

I'm going to get one of those nine-year-old Persian kids they use to make incredibly tiny knots in fine Bokhara rugs and just take her with me on all my fishing trips.

What I really needed was a fly-fishing how-to video narrated by Mister Rogers. This would give me advice about which direction to wind the reel and why I should never try to drive a small imported car while wearing waders. (Because when I stepped on the accelerator, I also stepped on the brake and the clutch.)

I rewound Mr. Squeaky and started over. I was supposed to keep my rod tip level and keep my rod swinging in a ninety-degree arc. When I snapped my wrist forward, I was giving one quick flick of a blackjack to the skull of a mugging victim. When I snapped my wrist back, I was sticking my thumb over my shoulder and telling my brother-in-law to get the hell out of here and I mean right now, buster. Though it wasn't explained with quite so much poetry.

Then I was told to try these things with a "yarn rod." This was something else I'd bought at the tackle shop. It looked like a regular rod tip from a two-piece rod, but had a cork handle. You run a bunch of bright-orange yarn through the guides and flip it around. It's supposed to imitate the action of a fly rod in slow motion. I don't know about that, but I do know you can catch and play a nine-pound house cat on a yarn rod, and it's great sport. They're hard to land, however. And I understand cat fishing is strictly catch-and-release if they're under twenty inches.

Then I went back to the television and heard about stance, loop control, straight-line casts, slack-line casts, stripping, mending, and giving myself enough room when practicing in the yard so I wouldn't get tangled in my neighbor's bird feeder.

After sixty minutes of video tape, seven minutes of yarn-rod practice, twenty-five minutes of cat fishing, and several beers, I felt I was ready. I picked up the fin tickler and laid out a couple of loops that weren't half bad, if I do say so myself. I'll bet I cast almost three times before making macramé out of my weight-forward Cortland 444. This wasn't so hard.

I also watched the advanced tape. But Squeaky had gone grad school on me. He's throwing reach casts, curve casts, roll casts, steeple casts, and casts he calls "squiggles" and "stutters." He's writing his name with the line in the air. He's pitching things forehand, backhand, and between his wader legs. And, through the magic of video editing, every time his hook-tipped dust kitty hits the water, he lands a trout the size of a canoe.

The video tape about trout themselves wasn't much use either. It's hard to get excited about where trout feed when you know that the only way you're going to be able to get a fly to that place is by throwing your fly box at it.

I must say, however, all the tapes were informative. "Nymphs and streamers" are not, as it turns out, naked mythological girls decorating the high school gym with crepe paper. And I learned that the part of fly fishing I'm going to be best at is naming the flys: Wooly Hatcatcher; Blue Wing Earsnag; Overhanging Brush Muddler; Royal Toyota Hatchback; O'Rourke's Ouchtail; and PJ's Live Worm-'n'-Bobber.

By now I'd reached what I think they call a "learning plateau." That is, if I was going to catch a fish with a fly rod, I either had to go get in the water or open the fridge and toss hooks at Mrs. Paul's frozen haddock fillets.

I made reservations at a famous fishing lodge on the Au Sable River in Michigan. When I got there and found a place to park among the Saabs and Volvos, the proprietor said I was just a few days early for the Hendrickson hatch. There is, I've learned, one constant in all types of fishing, which is: The time the fish are biting is almost but not quite now.

I looked pretty good making false casts in the lodge parking lot. I mean no one laughed out loud. But most of the other two thousand young professionals fishing this no-kill stretch of the Au Sable were pretty busy checking to make sure that their trout shirts were color coordinated with their Reebok wading sneakers.

When I stepped in the river, however, my act came to pieces. My line hit the water like an Olympic belly-flop medalist. I hooked four "tree trout" in three minutes. My backcasts had people ducking for cover in Traverse City and Grosse-Pointe Farms. The only thing I could manage to get a drag-free float on was me after I stepped in a hole. And the trout? The trout laughed.

The next day was worse. I could throw tight loops. I could sort of aim. I could even make a gentle presentation and get the line to lie right every so often. But when I tried to do all of these things at once, it was disaster. I looked like I was conducting "Flight of the Bumblebee" in fast forward. I was driving tent pegs with my rod tip. My slack casts wrapped around my thighs. My straight-line casts went straight into the back of my neck. My improved surgeon's loops looked like full Windsors. I had wind knots in everything, including my Red Ball suspenders. And two hundred dollars' worth of fly floatant, split shot, Royal Coachmen, and polarized sunglasses fell off my body and were swept downstream.

Then, *mirabile dictu*, I hooked a fish. I was casting some I-forget-the-name nymph and clumsily yanking it in when my rod tip bent and my pulse shot into trade-deficit numbers. I lifted the rod—the first thing I'd done right in two days—and the trout actually leaped out of the water as if it were trying for a *Field & Stream* playmate centerfold. I heard my voice go up three octaves, until I sounded like my little sister in the middle of a puppy litter, "Ooooo that's a boy, that's a baby, yessssssss, come to daddy, wooogie-woogie-woo." It was a rainbow, and I'll bet it was seven inches long. All right, five. Anyway, when I grabbed the thing, some of it stuck out both sides of my hand. I haven't been so happy since I passed my driver's-license exam.

So I'm a fly fisherman now. Of course I'm not an expert yet. But I'm working on the most important part of fly-fishing technique—boring the hell out of anybody who'll listen.

60 The Way it Looks from the Stern Seat.

A Meditation on the
Midlife Crisis and the Literature,
Psychology and Mystique of
Fly Fishing

Howell Raines

*Except for the suicide of Frank Forester in his thirties—a man whom even fly fishing
could not save—there's little in this intriguing essay about honest-to-goodness
midlife crises; but it was meant really to be about much more—the sources of our passion,
the happy exegesis of the act of fly fishing and its relationship to other sports, its history,
and much else. Howell Raines' concluding line neatly sums up
themes that have run through this entire book.*

—NL

The most widely read American fishing writer of the mid-nineteenth century was Henry W. Herbert, who was singled out by Edgar Allan Poe as a finalist in the category of having "written more trash than any man living." Herbert was born into a titled English family, but shortly after he finished Cambridge, he was given a small trust fund and exiled permanently to New York by his father for a breach of manners so profound that its exact nature has been scrubbed from the family history. The trust fund proved inadequate for the full support of Herbert's interests, which included womanizing, horse racing, and perfecting "the skill exerted in casting and managing a fly."

Herbert thought of himself as a serious novelist, but it was his fishing writing, under the pen name Frank Forester, that the public craved. Around 1845, when he was thirty-eight years old, Herbert fell into a notable funk. It lasted for thirteen years, culminating when a younger woman, who married him for his money, got a look at his bank book and took off. "This desertion seems to have broken his will," notes one of his biographers.

In 1858, Herbert invited all his friends to a banquet to be served on May 15, but only one person showed up, perhaps because Herbert did not send the invitations until May 14. The solitary guest spent the entire evening trying to talk Herbert out of his threatened suicide and thought he had just about succeeded when his host left the table and went into an adjoining room. There was a gunshot, and Herbert came back into the room, bleeding from a mortal chest wound, and said, "I told you I would do it."

I was intrigued, even relieved, when I ran across this tale in *McClane's New Standard Fishing Encyclopedia*. Clearly, I was not the first writer to see—or at least experience—a confluence between fly fishing and masculine angst in life's middle passage. Poor Henry W. Herbert had long ago explored the aesthetics of the sport and stumbled down the dark tunnels of midlife. Never mind that Poe said the man could not write. Like most geniuses, Poe was intolerant of those with lesser gifts, and besides, Edgar was not exactly a model of stability himself. In any event, Herbert's importance for our purposes is that he was one of a claque of propagandists who by the time of the Civil War had established the artistic and psychic superiority of fly fishing. Herbert's editor at the *Turf Register* in the

1830s, William Trotter Porter, put it this way: "Fly fishing has been designated the royal and aristrocratic branch of the angler's art . . . the most difficult, the most elegant, and to men of taste, by myriads of degrees the most exciting and pleasant mode of angling."

There are over five thousand books on fishing in the English language, and in a fair number of them, the authors wrestle with the question of why some people like to pull fish out of the water. Since this is the most extensive literature of any sport, we can conclude that the question is (1) not easy to answer and (2) capable of holding the interest of at least a fair portion of literate humankind.

The standard explanation is that people are drawn to fishing as a way of reenacting and presumably calming the "atavisic impulses" inherited from our hunter-gatherer ancestors. But this explanation does not answer what is really being asked by the person who turns to you at a cocktail party in New York upon hearing that you've just paid $800 to be flown to Jackson Hole and another $350 to have someone float you down the Snake River while you wave a $300 rod in the air and says, "Why do you like to fish?"

In my view, the people who fish do so because it seems like magic to them, and it is hard to find things in life that seem magical. Partly this magic resides in the physical sensation. Hitting a line drive or a tennis forehand or a golf shot produces the species of pleasure I'm trying to describe. Another way of thinking of this feeling is to imagine that cells scattered throughout the bone marrow and particularly in the area of the elbows—are having subtle but prolonged orgasms and sending out little neural whispers about these events.

For some people, including me, pulling on a fish generates a physical pleasure on the order of what I've described above. I think that's part of why I like to catch fish. But what is there about catching a fish that seems magical in the psychological sense? The appeal is the same as that which resides in pulling a rabbit out of a hat. We have reached into a realm over which we have no explainable mastery and by supernatural craft or mere trickery created a moment that is as phenomenal on the hundredth performance as on the first.

Fish in the water represent pure potential. If the water is not clear, we do not know if they exist at all. To get them to bite something connected to a line and pull them into our world is managing a birth that brings these creatures from the realm of mystery into the world of reality. It's a kind of creation.

Then there are the fish themselves. When I see fish coming through the water, they seem as sovereign and self-contained as beings from another planet, and beholding them engenders the same kind of fascination that I imagine I might feel if a spacecraft opened and I was able to look inside and see beings of a profoundly different sort swimming in light.

In an essay for *Trout* magazine, Kitty Pearson-Vincent, a photographer, was trying to convey the quality of this visual experience in declaring that "the fish is otherworldly." She added: "Trout are like dreams hovering in the elusive unconscious. In capturing one, if ever so briefly, before release, there is that sense of revelation occurring when one awakens in the night, snatching a dream from the dark portals of sleep."

There is also the shape of fish. There are certain people to whom the shape of fish is extremely satisfying to behold. If you do not think so, start looking at the number of fish you see in sculpture and paintings. It is one of the most satisfying and seminal shapes in creation, and there are some of us who need to see it a lot. My house is chock-a-block with fish drawings, fish ceramics and fish carvings from India, Africa, the Caribbean, and, of course, Minnesota, where the production of antique fish decoys is a thriving new industry. I have had to get more selective in my collecting because of the recent explosion in fish fashions. These days there is hardly a boutique or catalog without its array of fish earrings and fish T-shirts. The Kellogg Collection, a trendy furniture store in Washington, is offering a chest of drawers with a hand-painted fly-fishing scene. From Tiffany to the lowliest pottery shed, vast schools of trout, bass, sunfish, sharks, and sting rays swim across our dinner plates.

I am drawn to the more primitive kinds of fish art. But whether we are talking about a handcarved decoy from the North Woods or an Art Deco marlin on a Miami Beach hotel, it is important to remember that such objects exist because this shape swims eternally in the Anima Mundi, the oceanic common memory of mankind. For my part, as I reflect more deeply on the fish's history as a mythic symbol and religious icon, I begin to wonder if having fish shapes around me is a way to stay in touch with the ideas of Jesus without having to go near the people who do business in his name. Anyway, those are some of my guesses about why people fish.

Moving from the realm of speculation to that of fact, we know that New Stone Age Man invented the fishhook sometime around 8000 B.C. It was a hard thing to invent, if you ask me, which probably explains why Old Stone Age Man did not invent the fishhook in the 640,000 or so years he had to work on inventing tools. Let's face it, the club is easy compared to the fishhook.

The metal hook with a barb and an eye existed in Crete about 3400 B.C., and it was the Macedonians on the Astraeus River who invented the fly. They tied red wool and cock feathers to a hook to imitate an "impudent" buzzing insect favored by brown trout there, according to Aelian, a writer in the third century A.D. He said: "When the fish spies one of these insects on the top of the water, it swims quietly underneath it . . . [A]pproaching it, as it were, under the shadow, it opens its mouth and gulps it down, just as a wolf seizes a sheep, or an eagle a goose, and having done this it swims away beneath the ripple."

Observing this, the Macedonian fishermen dangled their flies at the end of six-foot lines affixed to sticks of equal length. "The fish being attracted by the color becomes extremely excited," Aelian wrote, "proceeds to meet it, anticipating from its beautiful appearance a most delicious repast; but, as with extended mouth it seizes the lure, it is held fast by the hook, and being captured, meets with a very sorry entertainment."

By the late Middle Ages, flies on the same principle were being tied in the British Isles and dangled over trout there with long poles. In the earliest British fishing writing, we see an emphasis on aesthetics, using light tackle and conducting oneself in an elevated style. That is clear in the chapter on fishing with flies that Charles Cotton, a London layabout, contributed to the 1676 edition of *The Compleat Angler*, a book first published in 1653 by his friend, the noted bait fisherman Izaak Walton.

The younger man properly honored Walton as a better writer and as his "father" as a fisherman. But Cotton is a far more important figure than Walton in developing the aesthetic sense that has dominated British and American fishing ever since. Cotton wrote that the most elegant way to catch trout was to fish "fine and far off" with a long pole, a light line of one to four horsehairs, and virtually weightless flies that drifted naturally on the surface. Ever since, fly fishermen have looked down on live-bait fishermen like Walton and their heavy lines. "He that cannot kill a trout on two [hairs], deserves not the name of angler," Cotton said.

With Cotton originated the idea that this kind of fishing had to involve physical grace, utilizing motions that blended with the gentle movements of breeze and current. But with a pole of fifteen to eighteen feet, Cotton could not make the elegant casting motion that developed with the shorter, highly flexible rods that began to appear in the early nineteenth century, along with reels and lines of greased silk. These made possible the distinctive buggy-whip effect gained from a rhythmic waving of the rod and the airy extension of a gradually lengthened line that settles to the water like a falling strand from a spider's web.

For over a century, the great breakthroughs in fly-fishing technology have occurred in the United States. In 1846, Samuel Phillippe of Easton, Pennsylvania, perfected the hexagonal rod, made by gluing together six long, triangular shaped splinters of Asian bamboo. In cross section, Phillippe's rod looked like this:

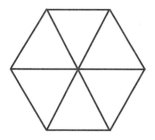

Because of the difficulty of shaving, fitting and gluing these long pieces of bamboo or cane, such rods are still the most expensive. But they were surpassed as casting and fish-fighting instruments, although not as art objects, by the next round of innovations. These came with the perfecting of fiberglass rods by Dr. A. M. Howald, a chemist from Perrysburg, Ohio, in 1948 and with the manufacture of graphite rods in the 1980s. Also, the introduction of a new coating material for fly lines, polyvinyl chloride, in 1949 made greased silk lines obsolete and ended the sinking problems that plagued my uncle Erskine.

As far as equipment goes, we are living in the Golden Age of Fly Fishing. Where there used to be only a couple of hundred truly expert fly fishermen in the United States, there are now thousands who could match the best practitioners in the history of the sport. Naturally, as in any group so large, some are jerks. All are snobs when it comes to what they really think about other forms of fishing.

That is because of the aesthetic principle at the core of fly fishing. It is the most beautiful way of trying to catch a fish, not the most efficient, just as ballet is the most beautiful way of moving the body between two points, not the most direct.

Fly fishing is to fishing as ballet is to walking.

It is interesting that many men come to fly fishing after they have been through other kinds of fishing, usually forms that involve powerful boats, heavy rods and brutally strong fish.

Perhaps this is because they are getting wiser and less hormonal. Or perhaps it is that as men get older, some of them develop holes in their souls, and they think this disciplined, beautiful and unessential activity might close those holes.

Acknowledgments

➤ "East Hampton, August 28, 1939" excerpted from *Fishing Came First* by John N. Cole. Copyright © 1989 by John N. Cole. Used by permission of Lyons & Burford, Publishers. ➤ "Mecca" by Nick Lyons. Copyright © 1970 by Nick Lyons. Used by permission of the author. ➤ "Tuna Fishing in Spain" is reprinted with permission of Charles Scribner's Sons, an imprint of Macmillan Publishing Company, from *Ernest Hemingway: Dateline Toronto*, edited by William White. Copyright © 1985 by Mary Hemingway, John Hemingway, Patrick Hemingway, and Gregory Hemingway. ➤ "Trout" from *Poems 1965-1975* by Seamus Heaney. Copyright © 1980 by Seamus Heaney. Reprinted by permission of Farrar, Straus & Giroux, Inc. ➤ "The Long Light" by Le Anne Schreiber. Originally appeared in *The Independent* (Columbia County, New York); reprinted by permission of the author. ➤ "Abe Lincoln Fished Here" by Lin Sutherland, copyright © 1990. ➤ "Mr. Theodore Castwell" by G. E. M. Skues. Copyright Seeley Service & Co., Ltd. The material taken from *Sidelines, Sidelights, and Reflections* by G. E. M. Skues. Copyright © 1947 by G. E. M. Skues. ➤ "Murder" from *Fishless Days, Angling Nights*. Copyright © 1954 by Alfred W. Miller. Copyright renewed © 1971 by Alfred W. Miller. Used by permission of Lyons & Burford, Publishers. ➤ "The Brakes Got Drunk" from *The Red Smith Reader* by Red Smith. Copyright © 1982 by Random House, Inc. Reprinted by permission of Random House, Inc. ➤ "Hairy Gertz and the Forty-Seven Crappies" from *In God We Trust, All Others Pay Cash* by Jean Shepherd. Copyright © 1966 by Jean Shepherd. Used by permission of Doubleday, a division of Bantam Doubleday Dell Publishing Group, Inc. ➤ Excerpt from *Nothing but Blue Skies* by Thomas McGuane. Copyright © 1992 by Thomas McGuane. Reprinted by permission of Houghton Mifflin Co./Seymour Lawrence. All rights reserved. ➤ "Fly Fishing Folly" by Ailm Travler. Originally appeared in *Uncommon Waters: Women Write About Fishing,* edited by Holly Morris (Seattle, WA; Seal Press, copyright © 1991 by Holly Morris). Reprinted with permission of the publisher. ➤ "A Fly-Fishing Primer" by P. J. O'Rourke, collected in *Seasons of the Angler*, edited by David Seybold (Weidenfeld & Nicholson, 1988); copyright © 1988 by P. J. O'Rourke. Used by permission of Grove/Atlantic, Inc. ➤ "A Meditation on the Midlife Crisis and the Literature, Psychology and Mystique of Fly Fishing," pp. 104-112, from *Fly Fishing through a Midlife Crisis* by Howell Raines. Copyright © 1993 by Howell Raines. Reprinted by permission of William Morrow & Company, Inc.